Disney
KNITS

Disney KNITS

Melinda Coss & Debby Robinson

GUILD PUBLISHING LONDON

This edition published 1987 by
Book Club Associates by arrangement
with Sidgwick & Jackson Limited

Reprinted 1988

Photography: Brenda Knight P.R.

Produced by the Justin Knowles Publishing Group,
9 Colleton Crescent, Exeter, Devon, England

Design: Vic Giolitto

Typeset by P&M Typesetting Ltd, Exeter, Devon

Printed in Italy by
New Interlitho

Contents

WALT DISNEY COPYRIGHT

The characters incorporated in the garments included in this book are copyright The Walt Disney Company, and the colours indicated on the graphs are those officially approved by the Company.

For reasons of time and the unavailability of suitable yarns, some of the finished garments illustrated on the pages that follow do not conform exactly to Disney preferred colours. However, to ensure that the characters you choose to knit are as authentic as possible, you should make every effort to match the colours of the yarns you use as closely as possible to the colours shown in the graphs.

In addition, to give your garment the final, authentic touch, when you have completed it, you should stitch the symbol "© Disney" using backstitch (*see* page 12). The ideal place on garments that have a single character motif is at the bottom and to one side of the motif. On garments with an all-over design, stitch the copyright logo at the lower left-hand side of the front.

TECHNIQUES

READING THE GRAPHS

Throughout the book full colour graphs illustrate the motifs to be incorporated into the garments; stitch symbols have been added where necessary. Each square on the graphs represents one stitch across – i.e., horizontally – and one row up – i.e., vertically. The graphs should be used in conjunction with the written instructions, which explain where and when to incorporate them. Always assume that you are working in stocking stitch unless otherwise instructed.

If you are not experienced in the use of graphs, remember that when you look at the flat page you are looking at a graphic representation of the right side of your knitting, that is, the smooth side of stocking stitch. For this reason, wherever possible, the graphs begin with a right side (RS) row so that you can see exactly what is going on as you knit. Knit rows are worked from right to left, purl rows from left to right.

If a design covers an entire garment or part of a garment such as a sleeve, the graph represents the whole knitting area, from selvedge to selvedge. When a graph is used for a motif that is worked on a one-colour background, it is boxed and the written instructions tell you exactly where this box slots into the work. It is vital that you work every stitch indicated within the border of this box, whether it is in base colour or contrast, to ensure that the motif is correctly positioned on the finished garment.

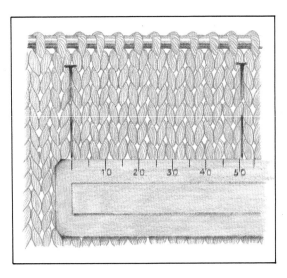

TENSION

Knitting is simply the process of making a series of interconnecting loops, the formation of which is completely under the knitter's control. Tension or gauge is the term used to describe the actual stitch size – its width regulating the stitch tension measurement, and its depth regulating the row tension measurement. Obtaining a particular tension is not a magical skill, denied to all but the initiated. It is a technicality, the controlling factor of which is the size of needles used by the knitter.

Since all knitting instructions are drafted to size using mathematical calculations that relate to one tension and one tension only, you must achieve the stated tension before you start work or you will have no control over the size of the finished garment. *This is the most important rule of knitting.*

At the beginning of every pattern a tension measurement is given, using a specific stitch and needle size – e.g., "using 5mm needles and measured over st st: 18 sts and 24 rows = 10cm square". You must work a tension sample using the same stitch and needle size as quoted. Cast on the appropriate number of stitches plus at least two extra, because edge stitches do not give an accurate measurement. When it is complete, lay the tension sample or swatch on a flat surface and, taking great care not to squash or stretch it, measure the tension, using a ruler and pins as shown.

If there are too few stitches, your tension is too loose. Use needles that are one size smaller to work another swatch. If there are too many stitches, your tension is too tight. Use needles that are one size larger to work another swatch.

Even if you have to change needle sizes several times, *keep working swatches until you get it right*. You save no time by skipping this stage of the work; if you do not get the correct tension, you risk having to undo an entire garment that has worked out to the wrong size. You may feel that a slight difference is negligible, but a tension measurement that is only a fraction of a stitch out in every centimetre will result in the garment being the wrong size, since each fraction will be multiplied by the number of centimetres across the work.

If you have to change your needle size to achieve the correct tension for the main stitch,

Use a ruler and pins to measure the tension of a sample piece of knitting.

remember to adjust, in ratio, the needles used for other parts of the garment that are worked on different sized needles. For example, if you are using one size smaller needles than are quoted for stocking stitch, use one size smaller needles than are quoted for the ribs.

Many people worry unnecessarily about row tension, changing their needle size even though they have achieved the correct stitch tension. Although important, row tension does vary considerably from yarn to yarn and from knitter to knitter. If your stitch tension is absolutely accurate, your row tension will be only slightly out. Nevertheless, keep an eye on your work, especially when working something like a sleeve that has been calculated in rows rather than centimetres, and compare it with the measurement chart in case it is noticeably longer or shorter.

The fairisle method of colour knitting can make a great deal of difference to your tension. If you are working a motif in fairisle on a one-colour background, take extra care with the tension, working as loosely as possible so that the motif area does not pull more tightly than the stitches around it so causing your work to pucker and the actual motif to become distorted. To avoid this, it is advisable to use the intarsia method wherever practical (*see* page 9).

TURNING

Turning is also sometimes called "working short rows", since this is precisely what is done. By turning the work mid-row and leaving part of it unworked, your piece of knitting is shaped, because one side has more rows than the

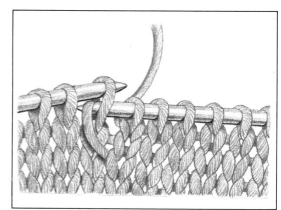

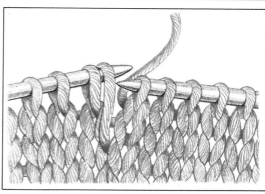

other. If the work is then cast off, the edge will slope, and this is, therefore, an ideal way to shape shoulders. Turning is not advisable if you are working complicated stitches or colour patterns, because the process of turning is likely to throw them out.

Unfortunately, holes tend to form at the turning points, even if care is taken. There is a way of overcoming this, and, although it appears complicated at first, it is well worth the effort of learning to master the technique. The method may be used on right or wrong side rows; here it is illustrated on the right side of stocking stitch.

1. Knit to the point where turning is indicated, but before doing so bring the yarn to the front of the work and slip the next stitch from the left-hand to the right-hand needle.
2. Put the yarn to the back of the work and return the slipped stitch to the left-hand needle.
3. Now turn the work and purl to the end.

Repeat the last three steps at every turning point. All the stitches must now be worked across, and so if the turned shaping is being worked immediately before casting off or knitting a seam, you should add an extra row. Work to the first stitch that has had a loop made

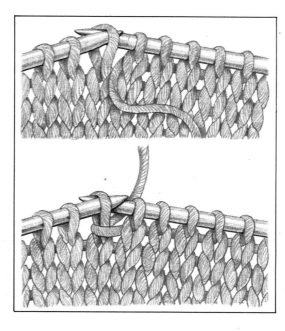

Right: to ensure that holes do not form at turning points, bring the yarn to the front of the work and slip the next stitch from the left-hand to the right-hand needle. Then put the yarn to the back of the work and return the slipped stitch to the left-hand needle before turning the work. Above right: add an extra row if you are working a turned shaping before casting off or knitting a seam.

around it by putting the yarn forward and then back as above. Then:

1. Slip this stitch from the left-hand to the right-hand needle.
2. Using the point of the left-hand needle, lift the loop up onto the right-hand needle, making an extra stitch.
3. Replace the two stitches on to the left-hand needle, making sure that they are not twisted, and knit them together.

Work to the next "looped" stitch and repeat the process. When this row is completed, the work may be continued as normal.

INTARSIA

Intarsia is the term used to describe the technique of colour knitting by which each separate area of colour is worked using a separate ball of yarn. The colours are not carried from one area to another as with fairisle knitting. Any design that involves large blocks of isolated colour that are not going to be repeated along a row or required again a few rows later should be worked in this way.

There is no limit to the number of colours that may be used on any one row, apart from that imposed by lack of patience or dexterity. Apart from the problem of getting into a tangle if there are too many separate balls of yarn hanging from the back of your work, you should also remember that every time a new ball of yarn is introduced and broken off after use, two extra ends are produced that will have to be secured when you are finishing the garment. When ends are left, always make sure that they are long enough to thread up so that they may be properly fastened off with a pointed tapestry needle. Do this carefully through the backs of the worked stitches so that the design on the right side of the work is not distorted. On no account should you knot the ends to secure them; as well as looking unsightly, the knots will invariably work themselves loose.

If only a few large, regular areas of colour are being worked, the different balls of yarn may be laid on a table in front of you while you work or kept separate in individual jam jars or even shoe boxes. This stops the wool getting into a tangle but requires careful turning at the end of every row so that the yarns do not become twisted.

The easiest method is to use small bobbins that hold each colour separately and hang at the back of the work. These may be bought

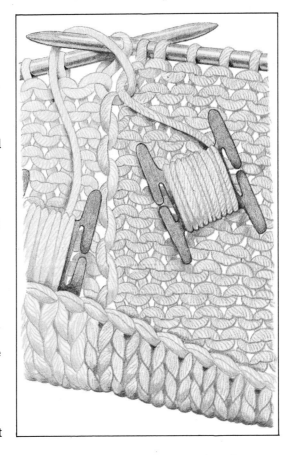

If you are using the intarsia method, twist the yarns firmly together when you change colours.

from most large yarn stores or made at home out of stiff card. They come in a variety of shapes, but all have a narrow slit in them to keep the wound yarn in place but allow the knitter to unwind a controlled amount as and when required. When winding yarn on to a bobbin, try to wind sufficient to complete an entire area of colour but don't overwind, as heavy bobbins will pull stitches out of shape.

When you change colour from one stitch to another, it is vital that you twist the yarns around each other before dropping the old colour and working the first stitch in the new colour. This prevents a hole forming. If you do not twist the yarns there is no strand to connect the last stitch worked in colour "A" to the first stitch worked in colour "B". Twist the yarns quite firmly to prevent a gap appearing after the work has settled.

FAIRISLE

The technique of colour knitting called "fairisle" is often confused with the traditional style of colour knitting that originated in the Fair Isles and took its name from those islands. Instructions that call for the fairisle method do not necessarily produce the multi-coloured, geometric patterns that are associated with the Fair Isle style of knitting. The technique is suitable for any style of work in which small repetitive areas of colour make the use of individual balls of yarn (intarsia method), impracticable.

Fairisle may be defined as knitting in which two colours are used across a row, the one not in use being carried at the back of the work until it is next required. This is normally done by dropping one colour and picking up the other with your right hand. If you are lucky enough to have mastered both the "English" and "Continental" methods of knitting, both hands may be used so that neither yarn has to be dropped. One colour is held in the left hand while the other colour is held in the right hand at all times. The instructions below, however, cover the more standard one-handed method and give the three alternative ways of dealing with the yarn not in use.

Stranding

Stranding is the term used to describe the technique by which the yarn not in use is simply left hanging at the back of the work until it is next needed. The yarn in use is then dropped and the carried yarn taken up, ready for action. This means that the strand or "float" produced on the wrong side of the work pulls directly on the stitches either side of it.

It is essential that the float is long enough to

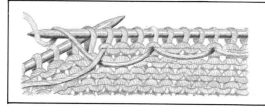

span the gap without pulling stitches out of shape and to allow the stitches in front of it to stretch and prevent them from puckering on the right side of the work. It is preferable to go to the other extreme and to leave a small loop at the back of the work rather than pulling the float too tightly.

If the gap to be bridged by the float is wide, the strands produced may easily be caught and pulled when the garment is put on or taken off. This may be remedied by catching the floats down with a few stitches on the wrong side of the work when you are finishing off the garment.

Weaving

With weaving the yarn being carried is looped over or under the working yarn on every stitch,

creating an up and down woven effect on the wrong side of the work. Since the knitter does not have to gauge the length of the floats, many people find that this is the easiest method of ensuring an even, accurate tension. Weaving does increase the chances of the carried colour showing through on to the right side of the work, however, and it tends to produce a far denser fabric, which is not always desirable, especially if a thick, warm fibre such as mohair is being used.

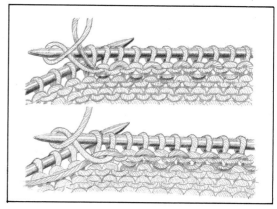

Stranding and weaving

Combining the two methods of stranding and weaving is invariably the most practicable solution to the problem of working perfect fairisle. Most designs have colour areas that contain varying numbers of stitches. If the gap between areas of the same colour is only a few stitches, then stranding will suffice, but if the float produced will be too long, weave the carried yarn in every few stitches. Should you be unsure about the length of float to leave, slip your fingers under one: if you succeed with ease, the float is too long.

The most difficult aspect of fairisle knitting is to get the tension correct. This does not depend on the stitch size so much as on the way you treat the carried yarn. This is why, when you work an all-over fairisle pattern, you should always knit a tension sample in fairisle, not in base colour stocking stitch, because the weaving or stranding will greatly affect the finished measurement of the stitches.

The most important rule to remember is that *the yarn being carried must be woven or stranded loosely enough to have the same degree of "give" as the knitting itself.* Unless you achieve this, the resulting fabric will have

---

Weaving the yarn creates a woven effect on the wrong side of your work.

If you use the stranding technique, leave a loop on the wrong side of the work rather than pull the yarn too tightly.

Be careful not to work too tightly with either the stranding or the weaving method.

no elasticity whatsoever, and very tight floats will buckle the stitches so that they lie badly on the right side of the work. On complicated designs, when more than two colours are used on a row, it may be necessary to carry more than one yarn at the back of the work. This should be avoided if at all possible, because ensuring that each colour is woven in at the correct place is time consuming and results in an even heavier fabric. In such instances it may be advisable to combine the methods of intarsia and fairisle.

BUTTONHOLES

A badly worked buttonhole can spoil the look of a garment, pulling the buttonband out of shape and looking loopy. It is also of no practical use if it is worked too tightly or, as more often happens, too loosely so that the buttons are not held.

Because finding buttons that are perfectly suited to the garment you are working can prove difficult, it is advisable to find the buttons before you work the buttonholes. The buttonhole size may then be adjusted slightly to suit the buttons rather than the other way round. The adjustment is easily made by casting off one or two stitches more or less than stated in the instructions – provided, of course, that there are enough stitches across the buttonband to accommodate such an alteration.

All the buttonholes used in this book are of the most basic, horizontal variety, worked over two rows. On the first row the required number of stitches is cast off at intervals corresponding to the distance between each button. On the next row the same number of stitches is cast on, immediately above those that were cast off on the previous row. If you use the thumb method of casting on, the first cast-on stitch often forms a loop unless it is worked with the yarn pulled very tightly on the needle. Alternatively, the work may be turned so that a two-needle method of casting on may be used to replace the cast-off stitches before turning the work back again and continuing the row normally until the next buttonhole point is reached.

When you work a buttonhole across ribbing, which is the most usual practice, keep in pattern throughout, although the casting off should be either knitwise or purlwise to give a firmer finish than a ribbed cast-off edge, which will be too elastic. Remember, all buttonholes should be a fraction too tight for their buttons when first completed, to allow for the inevitable stretching that occurs as a result of wear and tear.

MAKING A BOBBLE

Wherever the abbreviation MB appears in a pattern, it refers to a particular type of bobble, described below. If worked on a right side (RS) row the bobble will hang on the right side, if worked on a wrong side (WS) row, push the bobble through to the right side.

1. When the MB position on the row has been reached, make five stitches out of the next one by knitting into its front, then its back, front, back and front again before slipping the original stitch off the left-hand needle.
2. Turn the work and knit these five stitches only.
3. Turn the work, p2 tog, p1, p2 tog.
4. Turn the work, sl 1, k2 tog, psso.

Place this stitch on the left-hand needle, turn the work and continue as normal, the single stitch having been restored to its original position on the row.

SEAMS

After achieving the correct tension, the most important technique to master is the final sewing up of your knitting. This can make or break a garment, however carefully it may have been knitted, and is the reason the making up instructions in every knitting pattern should be followed precisely, especially the type of seam to be used and the order in which the seams are to be worked.

Before starting any piece of work always leave an end of yarn that will be long enough to complete a substantial part of the eventual seam, if not the whole thing. When you have worked a couple of rows, wind the end up and pin it to the work to keep it out of the way. If necessary, also leave a sizeable end when the work has been completed so that you may use it for seaming rather than joining in a new end, which may well work loose, especially at stress points such as welts.

The secret of perfect-looking seams is uniformity and regularity of stitch. When you join two pieces that have been worked in the same stitch they should be joined row for row. All work should be pinned first to ensure that the fabric is evenly distributed. When joining work that has a design on both pieces, take great care to match the colours, changing the colour you are using to sew the seam where necessary.

When you are using backstitch to join a seam and you are starting at the very edge of the work, close the edges with an overstitch before starting the row of backstitch. The finished seam should be even and perfectly straight, the two lower diagrams illustrating the front and back respectively of the completed seam.

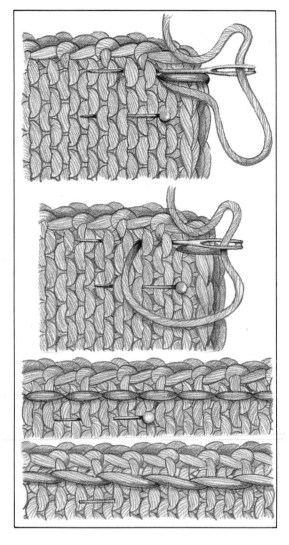

Backstitch

Pin the two pieces of work together, right sides facing, and make sure that the edges are absolutely flush. Always leave as narrow a seam allowance as possible to reduce unnecessary bulk. It is essential that the line of backstitches is kept straight and you should use the lines of the knitted stitches as a guide. All the stitches should be the same length, one starting immediately after the previous one has finished. The stitches should form a continuous straight line on the side of the work facing you. If the seam starts at the very edge of the work, close the edges with an overstitch, as shown, before working the backstitch:

1. Make a running stitch (maximum length 1cm), through both thicknesses of work.
2. Put the needle back into the work in exactly the same spot as before and make another running stitch, twice as long as the first.

3. Put the needle back into the work at the same point at which the previous stitch ended. Make another stitch, the same length.

Keep repeating stage 3 until the last stitch, which should be half as long as the other stitches to fill in the gap left at the end of the seam.

By keeping the stitch line straight and by pulling the yarn fairly firmly after each stitch, no gaps should appear when the work is opened out and the seam pulled apart.

This seam is suitable for lightweight yarns or where an untidy selvedge has been worked.

Flat seam

The expression "flat seam" is a slight contradiction in terms since it involves an oversewing action. However, when the work is opened out it will do so completely and lie quite flat, unlike a backstitched seam.

Use a blunt-ended tapestry needle to avoid splitting the knitted stitches. After pinning both pieces, right sides together, hold the work as shown. Pass the needle through the very edge stitch on the back piece and then through the very edge stitch on the front piece. Pull the yarn through and repeat the action, placing the needle through exactly the same part of each stitch every time. Always work through the edge stitch only. If you take in more than this, you will have a lumpy, untidy seam that will never lie flat.

When two pieces of stocking stitch are to be joined with a flat seam, do not work a special selvedge (such as knitting every edge stitch). Work the edge stitches normally but as tightly as possible, using the very tip of your needle. When you come to work the seam, place the tapestry needle behind the knots of the edge stitches and not through the looser strands that run between the knots, for these will not provide a firm enough base for the seam, which will appear gappy when opened out.

Flat seams are essential for garments made of heavy-weight yarns on which a backstitch would create far too much bulk. They should also be used for attaching buttonbands, collars and so forth, when flatness and neatness are essential. Borders, welts, cuffs and any other part of the garment where the edge of the seam will be visible should also be joined with a flat seam, even if the remainder of the garment has backstitched seams. In these instances, start with a flat seam until the rib/border is complete and then change over

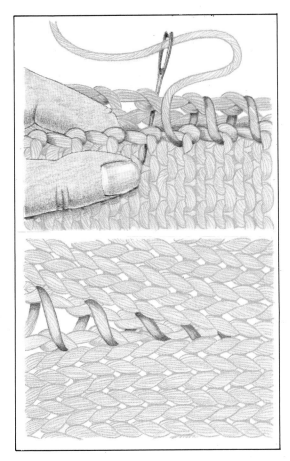

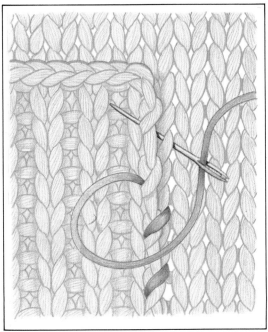

Far left: the diagrams show how you should hold the knitting to work a flat seam and how your work will look on the right side.

Left: use slip stitch to attach a pocket to a garment.

When you are slip-stitching a turned-in waistband, use the line of a row as a guide to produce a perfectly straight, horizontal line of stitches, which should not show through to the right side of the work. On pocket borders, use the line of stitches on the main work as a guide to produce a perfectly straight vertical line of stitches. Pass the tapestry needle through one strand of the main work stitch and then behind the knot of the border edge stitch, as for a flat seam.

KNITTED SHOULDER SEAMS

This method of joining is perfect for shoulders on which no shaping has been worked or on which the shaping has been worked by turning rows (*see* page 8). It creates an extremely neat, flat seam.

Because the two pieces to be joined must be

to backstitch, taking in a tiny seam allowance at first and then smoothly widening it, making sure that you do not suddenly increase the depth of the seam.

Slip stitch

If one piece of work is to be placed on top of another – for example, when turning in a double neckband, folding over a hem or attaching the edges of pocket borders – you should use slip stitch.

When you are turning in a neckband that has been cast off, place the needle through the cast-off edge and then through the appropriate stitch on the row where it was initially knitted up. It is essential that you follow the line of the stitch to avoid twisting the neckband. As you repeat the action, the visible sewn stitch runs at a diagonal.

The same rule applies when you sew down a neckband that has not been cast off but on which the stitches are held on a thread. The only difference is that the needle is placed through the actual held stitch to secure it. When each stitch has been slip-stitched down, the thread may be removed. This method results in a neckband with more "give" in it than one that has been cast off.

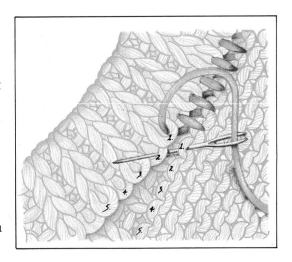

Use slip stitch to hold a double neck band in position.

The diagrams illustrate the three steps involved in knitting shoulder seams together. You must always have exactly the same number of stitches on the two pieces that are to be joined in this way.

worked stitch for stitch, they must both have exactly the same number of stitches. Even though the pattern will specify that you should have a certain number of stitches on your needles at this point, it is wise to double check the number you actually have, as it is very easy to lose or gain a stitch accidentally as you work.

The technique itself requires three needles. The stitches from the front and back are held on their respective needles, which should both be in your left hand, while in your right hand you should hold a third needle. This third needle should be larger than the others to help prevent the cast-off stitches being too tight. Holding more than one needle in the hand and trying to work through two stitches at a time without dropping them can seem very awkward at first, but, with a little practice, it will feel like normal knitting. Hold the needles so that the right sides of the work face one another and so that the stitches line up at corresponding intervals on the front and back needles. Work as follows:

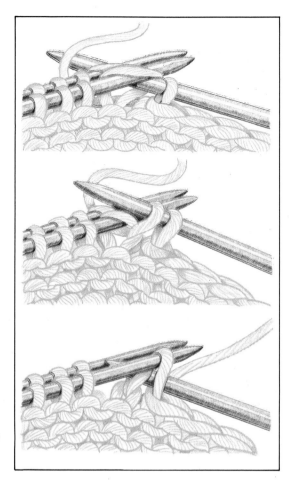

1. The point of the right-hand needle is put through the first stitch on the front needle and the first stitch on the back needle, with exactly the same action as a normal knit stitch but going through both simultaneously.
2. Pull a loop through to form a single stitch on the right-hand needle, slipping the old stitches off the left-hand needles.
3. Repeat steps 1 and 2 so that there are two stitches on the right-hand needle. The second stitch is then lifted over the first, as in normal casting off.

Step 3 should be repeated across all the stitches to be knitted together until one loop remains on the right-hand needle. Pull the yarn through this to secure it.

When you are knitting together a shoulder seam on a garment on which no neck shaping has been worked and on which the neck stitches have not been cast off, all the stitches on the back may be dealt with at the same time. Start to work the first shoulder together from the armhole to the neck edge, then cast off the back neck (if the pattern requires that they are cast off), without breaking the yarn, which may then be used to knit together the second shoulder seam from neck to armhole.

Although it is normally worked on the inside of the work to create an extremely neat, flat and durable seam, a knitted seam may also be worked with the wrong sides of the knitting

facing one another. This creates a decorative ridge on the right side of the work.

KNITTING UP STITCHES

The term "picking up" stitches is sometimes used instead of "knitting up" stitches, but it is rather a misleading phrase since it implies that the stitches are simply strands that have been pulled out around the edge of the work. This should never be done, for it produces uneven and untidy loops. The correct method is to use new yarn to create brand new stitches through the edge of the existing knitted fabric. This produces tidy, uniform stitches, and allows you to control the positioning of them.

As with working perfect flat seams, the preparation – i.e., the actual knitting – is the most important part of knitting up stitches. A firmly and neatly worked edge is essential for tidy knitting up. Always work edge stitches tightly, and if shaping has been worked – around a neckline, for instance – any decreases or increases should be worked one or two stitches in from the edge stitch wherever the pattern will allow. In this way the irregular, stretched stitches of the shaping are out of the way and the normally worked edge stitches can form the basis of the new stitches. Each new stitch should emerge from behind the knot of the edge stitch as this is the firmest part of the stitch. The strand between the knots will tend to stretch and should be used only when there is no alternative.

If you are working a colour pattern on a base colour, stop the pattern short a few stitches in from the edge so that the last few stitches are worked in base colour only. Knitting up from stitches of various colours will create an untidy line. When you are completing a piece of work that is to have stitches knitted up at a later stage, leave the yarn attached so that it may be used when required and so that you do not have to join in a new end of yarn, which will have to be secured.

When a pattern states exactly how many stitches are to be knitted up, if you are to work them in a stitch for which you have not worked a separate tension sample – e.g., rib when the pattern has required you to work a tension sample over stocking stitch – it is worthwhile to work a few knitted up stitches as a test before beginning the knitting-up proper since rib tension varies compared with stocking stitch.

If you find it difficult to distribute the number of stitches that are to be knitted up, divide your work into halves and then into quarters (and even eighths if it is a long edge), and mark these points with pins. Apportion the number of stitches equally among these sections. If they do not divide equally, use any extra stitches where they might be needed, such as at seam edges. Never distribute the stitches as you go along as this will invariably result in an uneven effect, with some areas bunched with too many stitches and others stretched with too few.

Once the edge has been prepared, hold the work with the right side towards you. Hold the yarn at the back of the work so that the stitches may be pulled through to the front. This may be done either with the needle you intend to use for the first row or, more easily, with a crochet hook. Use a crochet hook that will slip easily through the base stitch to catch the yarn and pull it through to the right side of the work where it is then slipped on to the needle holding the new stitches. Pull the yarn tight. The holding needle should be one or two sizes smaller than the size quoted for the actual knitting up to reduce the stitch size on the first row, thus creating a neater finish. Change to the correct needle size on your second row. The first row of a band or border that is to be ribbed may also be either knitted or purled as this, too, creates a smaller stitch than an initial

row of ribbing. Knitting this row with the right side facing you gives a smooth, inconspicuous row. If you purl this row, a ridge will be formed on the right side of the work, which will neaten the knit-up edge in a more ornamental way. Ribbing should then continue as normal.

If stitches are held between two areas of knitted-up stitches, as they may often be at the centre front edge of a crew neck, slip these stitches on to another needle and then knit them on to the holding needle. This will save you from having to break the yarn; slip the held stitches on to the holding needle and join in the yarn again to knit up further stitches. It is also advisable to knit up a stitch from the loop at the beginning and the end of any set of stitches that have been cast off or are on a holder. These are stress points and often become stretched, and an extra stitch will prevent a hole forming.

If you are using a set of double-pointed needles to knit around some necklines, the same rules apply, but the stitches that are knitted up must be equally distributed among the number of needles in use, leaving one needle free for the working.

SHOULDER PADS

The type of knitted shoulder pad for which instructions are given in the pattern for the Seven Dwarfs Cardigan (page 78) may be adapted for use in any garment, provided you allow for different thicknesses of yarn by altering the number of stitches.

Once knitted, the straight part of the pad should be turned back on itself to halve its depth and create a thicker edge. Slip stitch this into position.

The most important aspect of knitted shoulder pads is the way they are attached to the garment so that they sit correctly and do not pull the fabric out of shape. Do not turn the garment inside out. Fold the pad in half and slip it inside the garment, ensuring that the folded line corresponds to the line of the shoulder seam and the thick edge lies along the line of the armhole seam. Hold the garment up so that

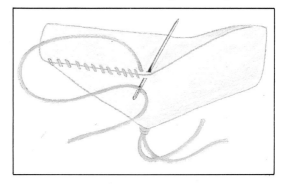

Turn the straight part of a knitted shoulder pad back on itself and slip stitch it into position.

Pin a shoulder pad in position before attaching it at the shoulder and armhole seams only.

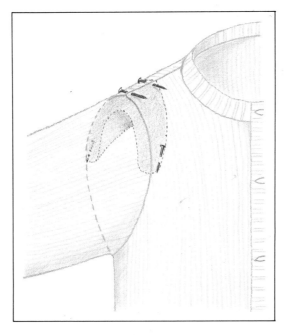

Satin stitch

Satin stitch is used to "in-fill" areas such as eyes. It is formed by working straight stitches, very close to one another, over the length of the area to be covered.

Backstitch

Outlines are worked in backstitch, which should be worked in exactly the same way as the stitch used for seams (*see* page 12). When you are working a curve, try to make very small stitches to ensure a continuous line.

FRINGES

A row of fringing adds the classic finishing touch to scarf ends and may be executed with the help of a crochet hook.

Because many lengths of yarn must be cut to a uniform length, find an object, such as a book, which the yarn may be wrapped around over and over again before cutting it along one side. The lengths produced should be two-and-a-half times longer than the required fringe length, for the knotting takes extra yarn and it is often necessary to trim the ends to produce a really straight line of fringes. Decide how many fringes you require and mark their positions on the cast-off and cast-on edges of the scarf.

Take several strands of yarn, depending on how fat you want the fringes, hold them flush with each other and fold them in half. With the right side of the work facing you, put the crochet hook through the edge and pull the fold point of the fringe through to form a loop on the wrong side of the work. Now put the crochet hook through the loop to pull the fringe ends up and through it. Pull this knot firmly, but not too tightly. When the whole row is complete, trim to the required length.

it takes its own weight, as it will do when worn, and pin the pad in position through the right side of the garment. Only when it is firmly positioned should the garment be turned inside out and the pad stitched in place.

The point of the pad should be attached to the shoulder seam and the two ends of the thick edge should be sewn to the armhole seam. Attach the pad at these three points only. Never attach a pad to the knitted fabric itself as this will pull the stitches out of shape and be visible on the right side of the work.

EMBROIDERY

To achieve the detail necessary for the facial features of some of the characters incorporated into the garments, simple embroidery stitches have been added after the knitting has been completed. You may find it helpful roughly to sketch on to the fabric, using tailor's chalk or lines of very small pins, the position and outline of the embroidery.

Right: when you embroider the facial features of some of the character motifs, use satin stitch for solid areas such as eyes and backstitch for outlines.

Far right: the three stages of knotting a fringe.

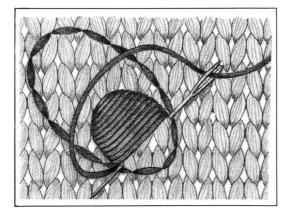

BIG BAD WOLF WOMEN'S SWEATER

An oversized, roll-neck raglan in a tweedy, aran-weight wool, with that bane of the Three Little Pigs, the Big Bad Wolf, looming menacingly on the front!

Materials
Melinda Coss aran tweed wool – base colour: 800gm; contrasts: less than 25gm of each of the seven colours, matched exactly to the graph.

Needles
One pair of 4½mm and one pair of 5½mm needles; a set of double-pointed 4½mm needles.

Tension
Using 5½mm needles and measured over st st: 16 sts and 24 rows = 10cm square.
N.B. Make every effort to keep your tension the same when working the colour motif. Do not carry the base colour behind the motif.

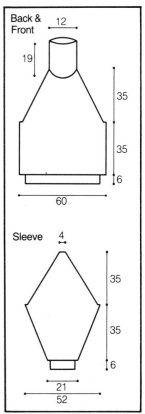

Back

Using base colour and 4½mm needles, cast on 96 sts.

Row 1: *k2, p2, rep from * to end. Keep rep this row to form double rib for 6cm, ending on a WS row. Knit the next row, inc into every 16th st (102 sts). Now change to 5½mm needles and cont in st st until the work measures 41cm, ending with a RS row.

Shape raglan: cast off 2 sts at beg of next 2 rows. Next row: purl. Row 2: k3, sl 1, k1, psso, k to last 5 sts, k2 tog, k3. Keep rep the last 2 rows until 22 sts remain. Work 3 rows straight. Cast off.

Front

As for back until 6 rows of st st have been worked.

Next row (RS): k8, k the first row from the graph, k to end. Cont working graph in this position until it is complete (meanwhile working raglan shaping throughout), then cont in base colour only. When raglan shaping has reduced to 34 sts **shape neck**: next row (WS) p12 sts, cast off 10 sts, p to end. Cont with this set of sts, leaving others on a holder. Dec 1 st at neck edge on the next 4 rows, meanwhile cont raglan shaping as before. Now work the neck edge straight and cont shaping raglan until 2 sts remain. Work 2 rows straight. P2 tog and pull yarn through remaining st to secure. Return to the other side of the neck, joining in yarn at neck edge. Work to match the first side.

Sleeves

Using base colour and 4½mm needles, cast on 36 sts and work in double rib for 6cm. Change to 5½mm needles and cont in st st, inc 1 st at each end of next and every following 3rd row until you have 90 sts. Work straight until the sleeve measures 41cm, ending with a RS row.

Shape raglan: as for back until 8 sts remain. Work 2 rows straight and then cast off.

Collar

Join all raglans with a flat seam. Using the set of double-pointed 4½mm needles and with the RS of work facing you, knit up 104 sts evenly around neckline. Knit the first row and then work in double rib until the collar measures 19cm. Cast off in rib.

Making up

Join remaining seams with a flat seam throughout.

BAMBI TEENAGERS' SWEATER

Materials
Melinda Coss 6-ply mercerized cotton – green: 450/500gm; white: 150/150gm; pink 25/25gm; contrasts: less than 25gm of each of the six colours, matched exactly to the graph.

Needles
One pair of 3mm and one pair of 3¾mm needles.

Tension
Using 3¾mm needles and measured over st st: 22 sts and 29 rows = 10 cm square.

N.B. Make every effort to keep your tension the same when working the colour motif. Do not carry the base colour behind the motif.

A delicate party sweater with a slightly scooped neck and raglan sleeves, quoted in sizes petite/small throughout. Knitted in a mercerized cotton in sugared almond colours, the sweater features Bambi in a shower of white bobbles.

Back
Using 3mm needles and white, cast on 88/98 sts.

Row 1: * k1, p1, rep from * to end. Keep rep this row to form single rib. Work 3 rows white in all, then 2 rows pink, 4 rows white, 2 rows pink. Change back to white and rib until work measures 6cm, ending with a WS row.

Next row: change to green and knit, inc into every 14th/16th st (94/104 sts). Change to 3¾mm needles and cont in st st, working from the graph. Omit the Bambi motif but work all bobbles (i.e., those indicated by "X" as well as "O"), in white, as indicated on the graph (see Techniques page 11). Break off yarn after completing each bobble; do not carry the yarn at the back of the work. Because two sizes have been superimposed on the same graph, you should omit bobbles that fall very near to the edge of the size you are working. Cont working from the graph throughout. When armholes are reached (work measuring approx 29/31cm), ending on a WS row, **shape raglan**: cast off 2 sts at beg of next 2 rows. Now dec 1 st each end of every 3rd row until 50/54 sts remain. Work 1 row straight. Cast off.

Front
As for back but work the Bambi motif and omit the bobbles represented by "X". Work graph throughout. Shape the raglan as for the back and when 62/66 sts remain **shape neck**: work 20/22 sts, cast off 22 sts, work to end. Cont with this set of sts, leaving the other sts on a holder. (Dec at raglan edge as before, throughout.) Dec 1 st at neck edge on every row until 12/7 sts remain. Now dec 1 st at neck edge on every alt row until 2 sts remain. Work straight for 1 row. Work 2 tog and secure by pulling yarn through the remaining st. Return to held sts, joining in yarn at neck edge and shaping to match.

Sleeves
Using 3mm needles and white, cast on 40/44 sts and work the rib exactly as for the back, ending on a WS row.

Next row: change to green and knit, inc into every 5th st (48/52 sts). Now change to 3¾mm needles and cont in st st, inc 1 st each end of every 6th row until you have 78/86 sts. Work straight until the sleeve measures 41/43cm, ending with a WS row. Now start working the bobbles from the sleeve graph and simultaneously start to **shape raglan**: cast off 3/2 sts at beg of next 2 rows. Now dec 1 st each end of every alt row until 12 sts remain. Work 3/1 rows straight. Cast off.

Neckband
Join raglan seams, excepting the right back sleeve, with a narrow backstitch. Using 3mm needles, white yarn and with RS of work facing, knit up 48/52 sts across the back neck, 10 sts over the sleeve top, 16 sts down the side of the neck, 22 sts across the front, 16 sts up the other side and 10 sts across the other sleeve top (122/126 sts). Purl the first row and then work in single rib for 2 rows. Change to pink and rib 2 rows. Return to white, rib 3 rows and cast off in rib.

The symbols "X" and "O" on the graphs on pages 21 and 23 indicate that bobbles should be worked at those points; see Making a bobble, page 11.

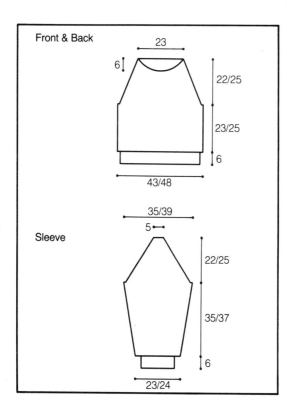

Front & Back
23
6
22/25
23/25
6
43/48

Sleeve
35/39
5
22/25
35/37
6
23/24

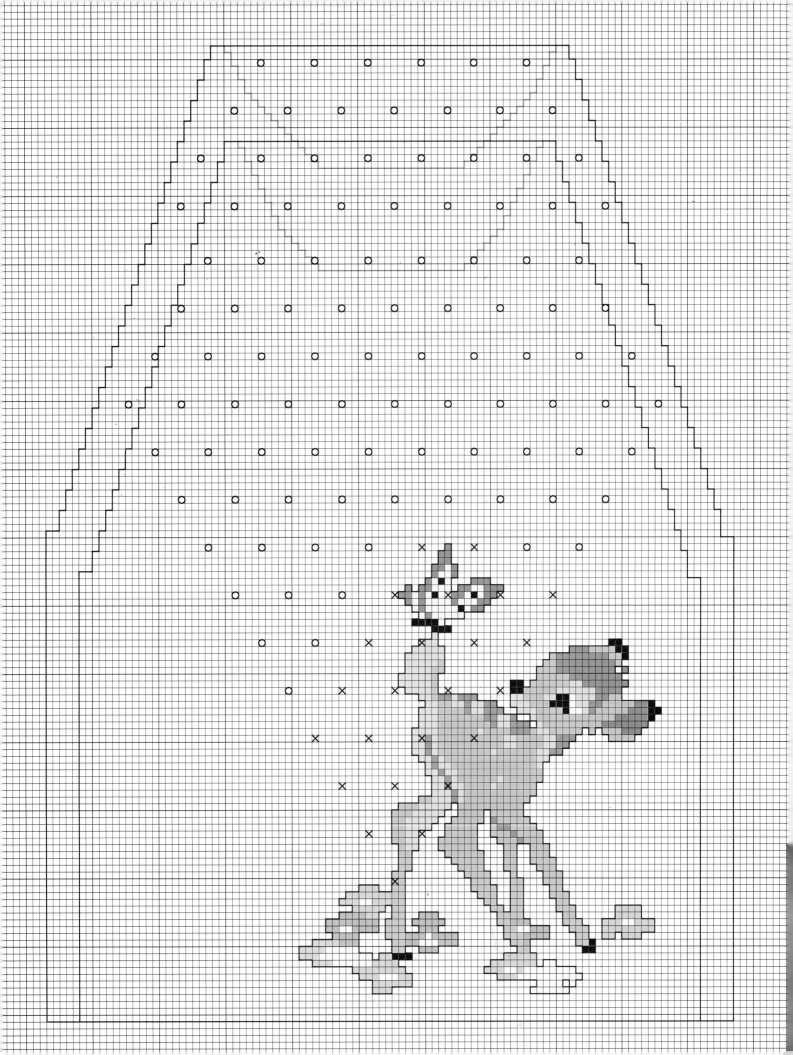

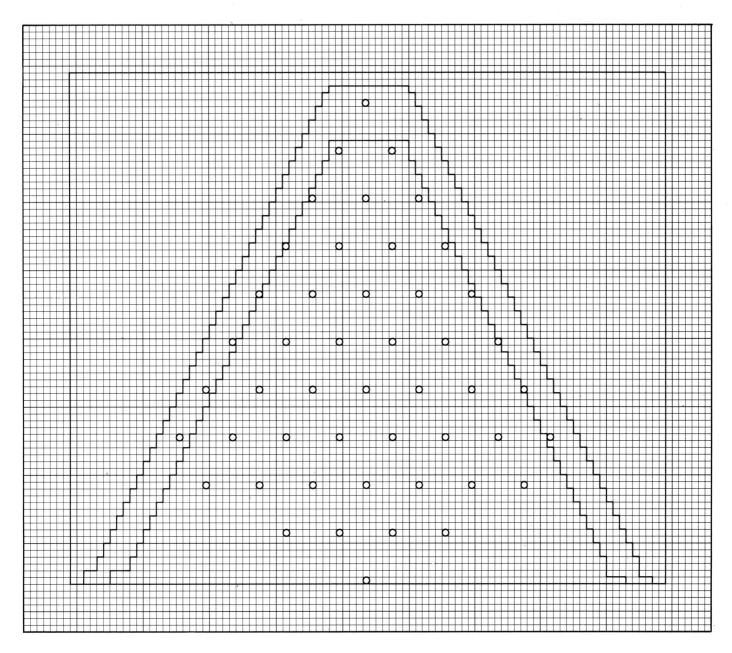

Making up

Join all ribbed parts with a flat seam, using a
narrow backstitch for the st st parts. Secure all
bobble and motif ends taking great care not to
pull any sts out of shape.

23

LADY AND THE TRAMP WOMEN'S SWEATER

A tunic-shaped, one-size sweater, in double knitting wool. Worked in stocking stitch, it has a moss stitch trim, including a neat little collar. The hero and heroine of Walt Disney's classic are portrayed on the front.

Materials
Melinda Coss DK wool – turquoise: 600gm; contrasts: less than 25gm of each of the 10 colours, matched exactly to the graph.

Needles
One pair 4mm and one pair 3¼mm needles.

Tension
Using 4mm needles and measured over st st: 24 sts and 32 rows = 10 cm square.
N.B. Make every effort to keep your tension the same when working the colour motif. Do not carry the base colours behind the motifs.

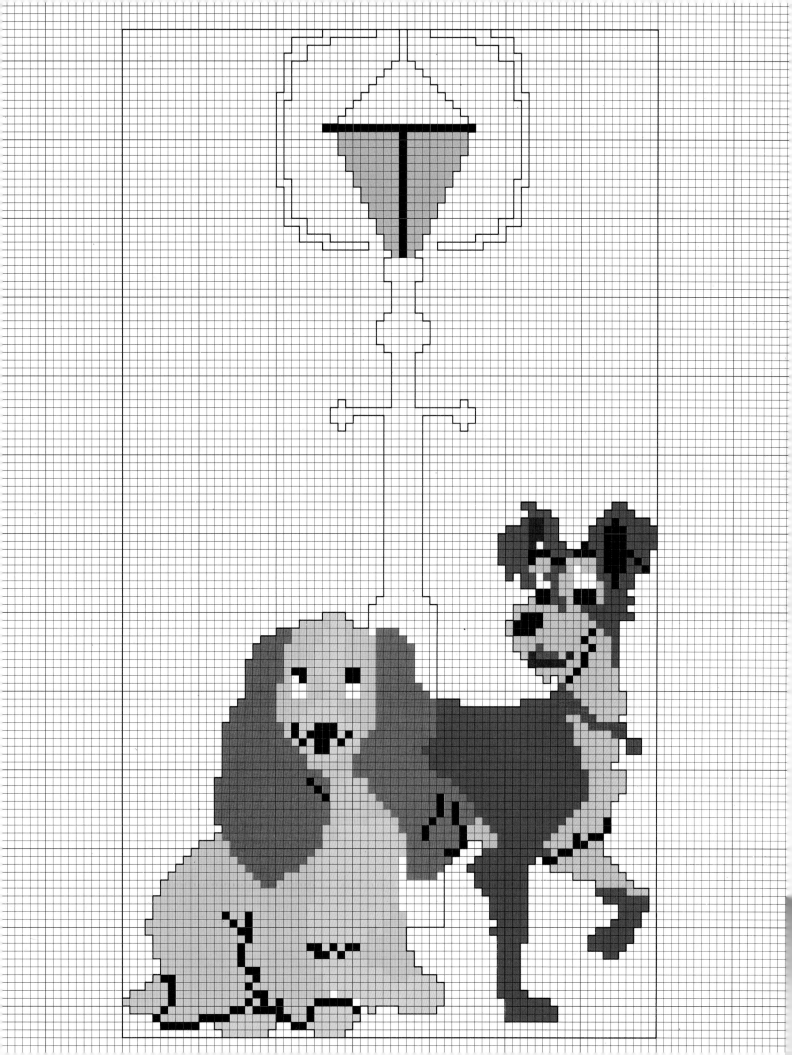

Back

Using 3¼mm needles and base colour, cast on 148 sts.

Row 1: *k1, p1, rep from * to end. Row 2: *p1, k1, rep from * to end. Keep rep these 2 rows to form moss st. When work measures 3cm, change to 4mm needles and cont in st st until work measures 80cm. Leave sts on a spare needle.

Front

As for back until work measures 13cm, ending with a WS row.

Next row: k39, k the first row of the graph, k to end. Cont working the graph in this position until it is complete. Now cont in base colour until the work measures 70cm. **Shape neck**: work 64 sts, cast off 20 sts, work to end. Cont with this set of sts, leaving the others on a holder. Dec 1 st at neck edge on every alt row until 54 sts remain. Work straight until this side is as long as the back. Leave sts on a holder. Return to the other side of the neck and shape to match. Leave sts on a holder.

Sleeves

Using 3¼mm needles and base colour, cast on 50 sts.

Row 1: *k1, p1, rep from * to end. Keep rep this row to form single rib for 4cm, ending on a WS row.

Next row: knit, inc into every 8th st (56 sts). Now change to 4mm needles and cont in st st, inc 1 st each end of every 4th row until you

have 110 sts. Work straight for 2 rows. Cast off loosely.

Collar

Using 3¼mm and base colour, cast on 140 sts and work in moss st for 10cm. Cast off in pattern.

Making up

Knit one shoulder seam tog, cast off the 40 back neck sts, loosely, knit second shoulder seam tog (*see* Techniques, pages 13-14). Open out the body and pin the sleeves in position, taking care not to bunch or stretch them. Sew with a flat seam. Join the side and sleeve seams with a flat seam but start the side seams where the moss st welt finishes so that there are 3cm vents either side of the finished garment.

Join the side edges of the collar to a depth of 1cm to make it stand very slightly, and place this seam to the centre front of the neck. Attach around the neck with a flat seam.

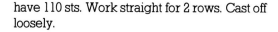

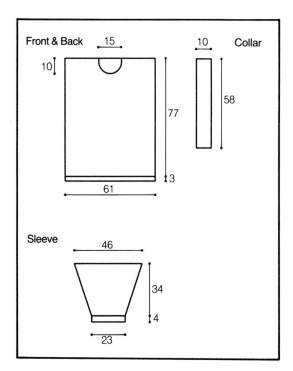

Front & Back   15
10
77
61
3

Collar   10
58

Sleeve   46
34
4
23

CRUELLA DE VIL WOMEN'S DRESS

The evil Cruella, scourge of 101 Dalmatians, is featured on this turtle-neck dress, which uses both aran-weight wool and mohair for the motifs.

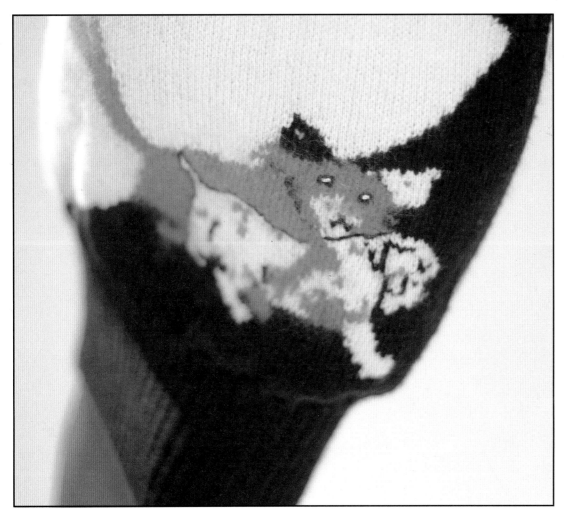

Materials
Melinda Coss aran-weight wool – black: 450gm; white: 400gm; dark red and scarlet: 50gm each; grey, khaki and fawn: less than 25gm each. Melinda Coss mohair – less than 25gm each of mink, brown, ginger, orange and turquoise, matched exactly to the graphs. Silver ribbon: less than 25gm.

Needles
One pair of 4mm and one pair of 5mm needles; a set of double-pointed 4mm needles.

Tension
Using 5mm needles and measured over st st: 18 sts and 23 rows = 10cm square.
N.B. Make every effort to keep your tension the same when working the colour motifs. Do not carry the base colour behind the motifs.

Front
Using 4mm needles and black, cast on 74 sts. Row 1: *k1, p1, rep from * to end. Keep rep this row to form single rib for 20cm, ending on a RS row. Purl the next row, inc into every 3rd st (98 sts). Now change to 5mm needles and cont in st st, working from graph, ignoring the line running across Cruella, which relates to the back only. When the armhole point is reached, cast off 2 sts at beg of these 2 rows and cont to neck shaping point. **Shape neck**: work 34 sts, cast off 26 sts, work to end. Cont with this set of sts, leaving others on a holder. Now dec 1 st at neck edge on every row until 26 sts remain. Put sts on a holder. Return to the other set of sts, joining yarn in at neck edge. Shape to match. Leave sts on a holder.

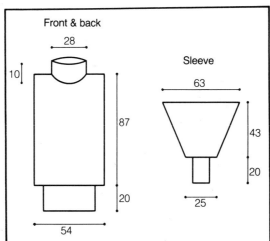

The graph on pages 28 and 29 is for the front of the dress.

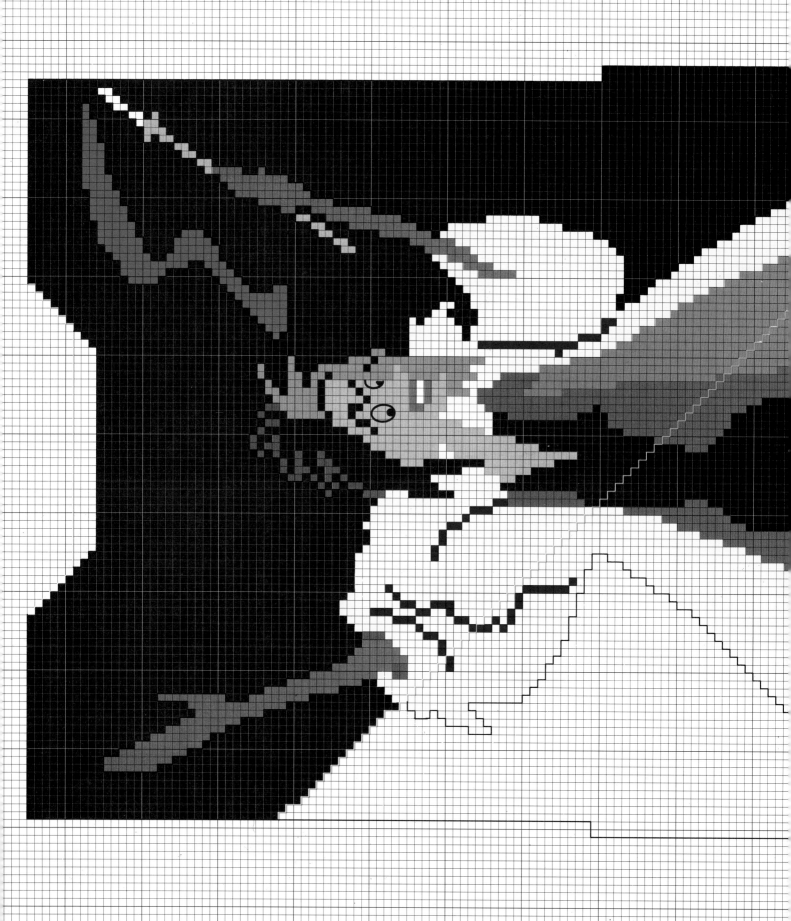

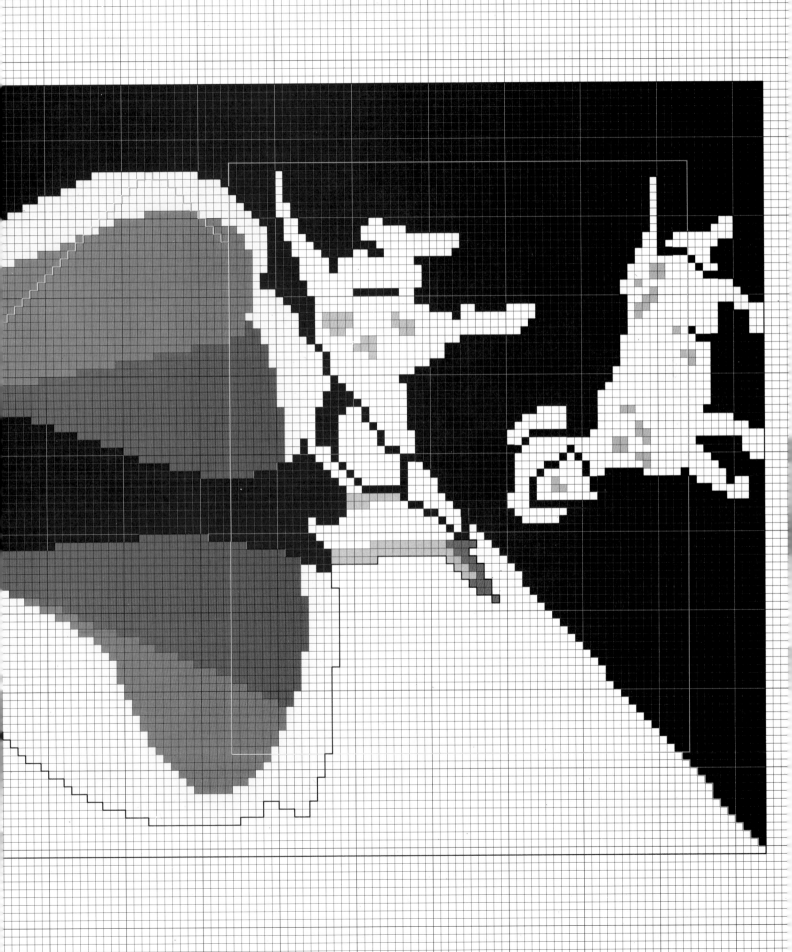

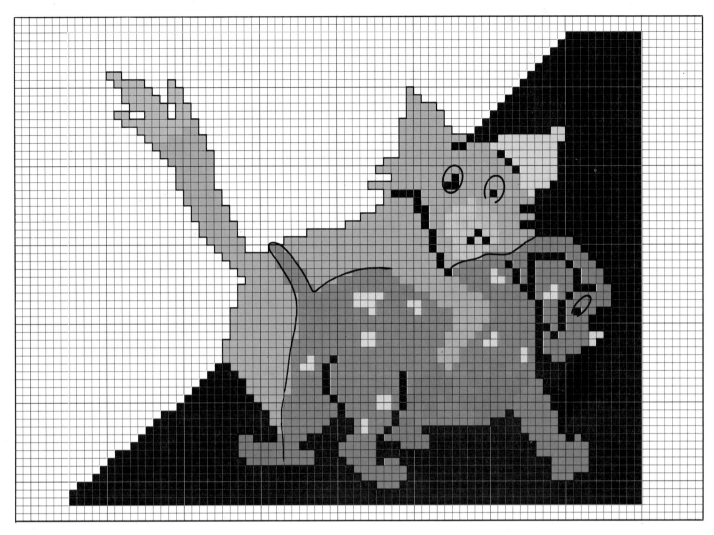

Back

As for the front but working plain st st in base
colours only for 9 more rows, after the inc row
(refer to backview photograph).

Row 11 (RS): k11, k the first row of cat graph, k
to end. Cont working the graph in this position
until it is complete. Now cont in st st in base
colours only, following the dividing line,
marked on graph but omitting Cruella. Shape
armholes as on front. When 195 rows have
been worked **shape neck**: work 31 sts, cast off
32 sts, work to end. Cont with this set of sts,
leaving others on a holder. Dec 1 st at neck
edge on every row until 26 sts remain. Leave
sts on a holder. Return to the other set of sts,
joining in yarn at neck edge. Shape to match
first side. Leave sts on a holder.

Sleeves

Using black and 4mm needles, cast on 50 sts
and work in single rib for 20cm, ending with a
WS row. Knit the next row, inc into the first and
every following 5th st (59 sts). Now change to
5mm needles and cont in st st, working from
the sleeve graph (page 33). Work the dog only
on the right sleeve and the smoke only on the
left, and inc 1 st each end of every 5th row.
When you have 95 sts cont straight to the length
shown. Cast off loosely.

Neckband

Knit both shoulder seams tog (*see* Techniques,
pages 13-14). Using double-pointed 4mm
needles and black, knit up 48 sts around the
back neck and 58 sts around the front. Knit the
first row and then work in single rib for 10cm.
Cast off loosely, in rib.

Making up

Open out the body and pin the sleeves in
position, distributing them evenly, each side of
the shoulder seams, and avoiding any
bunching. Attach with a flat seam and then join
side and sleeve seams likewise. Embroider the
outline of the dog and the dog's eye and cat's
eyes, as illustrated, using backstitch.

The cat graph should be
incorporated only into the
back of the dress.

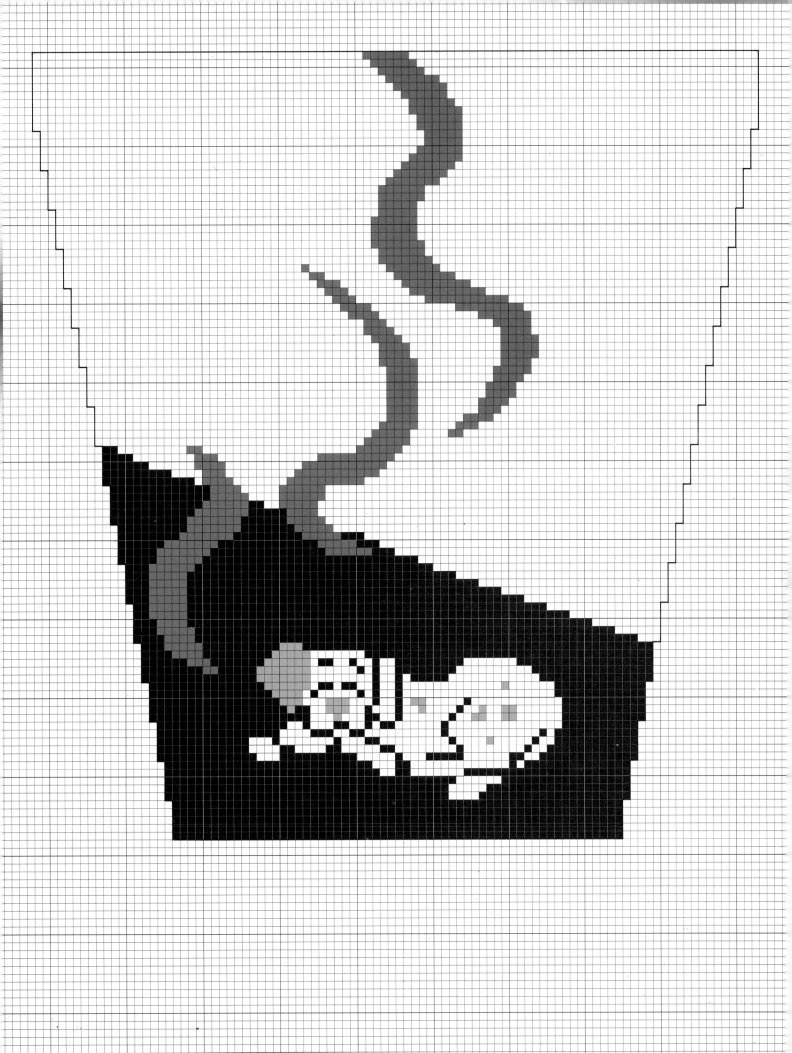

DAISY DUCK HAT, SCARF AND GLOVES SET

A warm combination of hat and scarf, worked in double knitting wool, with gloves in 4 ply. The colours of the motifs on the hat and gloves are echoed in the multi-coloured fringes of the scarf.

Materials
Base colour: hat: 100gm Melinda Coss DK; scarf: 250gm Melinda Coss DK; gloves: 50gm Melinda Coss 4 ply. Contrasts: less than 25gm of each colour, matched exactly to the graph.

Needles
A set of double-pointed 4mm needles for the hat; one pair of 4mm needles for the scarf; a set of double-pointed 3¼mm needles for the gloves.

Tension
Using DK yarn, 4mm needles and measured over st st: 22 sts and 32 rows = 10cm square; using 4-ply yarn, 3¼mm needles and measured over st st: 28 sts and 36 rows = 10cm square.
N.B. Make every effort to keep your tension the same when working the colour motif. Do not carry the base colour behind the motif.

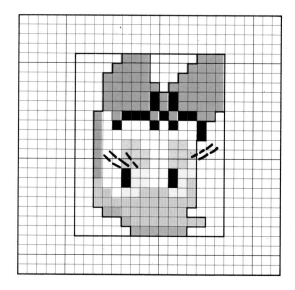

HAT
Using double-pointed 4mm needles and base colour, cast on 116 sts and work in rounds of single rib for 4cm. Now cont in st st, working straight until the work measures 9cm from the beg. Next round: k58, k the first row from the graph, k to end. Cont working the graph in this position until it is complete. Now cont in base colour only. Work 2 rows straight and then divide the sts into 4 groups with a marker before every 29th st. These 4 sts are the axial sts. Dec 1 st each side of each axial st on the next round (8 sts in all), and every following 8th round until 66 sts remain. Now dec 1 st each side of each axial st on every 4th round until 6 sts remain. Work 4 more rounds and then thread the yarn through the remaining sts, draw them up and secure them on the inside of the hat.

SCARF
Using 4mm needles and base colour, cast on 72 sts.
Row 1: *k1, p1, rep from * to end. Keep rep this row to form single rib. Work straight until the scarf measures 140cm. Cast off knitwise.

Fringes
The fringes are worked in the motif colours (excluding black) and are attached to the scarf alternately with base colour fringes, giving a total of 20 fringes along each end (*see* Techniques, page 16).

GLOVES
Right hand
Using a set of double-pointed 3¼mm needles, cast on 42 sts and work in single rib for 5cm. Next row: knit, inc into every 7th st (48 sts). Cont in st st. Work 4 more rounds. Now **work thumb gusset**: 5th round: k2, m1, k1, m1, to end. Work 3 more rounds. 9th round: k2, m1, k3, m1, k to end. Work 3 more rounds. 13th round: k2, m1, k5, m1, k to end. 14th round: k to last 18 sts of the round, work the first row of the

graph, k to end. Work the graph in this position until it is complete. Cont in base colour only. Meanwhile cont inc 2 sts every 4th round as set, 6 times (60 sts).
Work 8 rounds without shaping. Divide for thumb: k1, slip the next 14 sts onto a thread, cast on 5 sts, k to end. Work 14 more rounds without shaping.
First finger: k8, slip next 37 sts onto a thread, cast on 2 sts, k last 6 sts (16 sts now on needle). Divide sts onto 3 needles and work 25 rounds or more, according to finger length required. Next round: k2 tog all around. Work 1 round without shaping and then draw yarn through remaining sts and secure.
Second finger: k the next 6 sts of the round, cast on 2 sts, k last 7 sts of round and knit up 2 sts from the base of the first finger where the 2 sts were cast on (17 sts). K approx 31 rounds, to suit. Shape tip as for first finger.
Third finger: k next 6 sts of round, cast on 2 sts, k last 6 sts of round, knit up 2 sts from the base of the 2nd finger (16 sts). Work as for first finger.
Fourth finger: k remaining 12 sts of the round, knit up 2 sts from the base of the third finger. Knit approx 21 rounds, to suit. Shape tip as for first finger.
Thumb: k 14 sts which had been held, knit up 5 sts from the cast on sts. Divide between 3 needles. Work approx 23 rounds, to suit. Shape tip as for first finger.

Left hand

As for right hand until the start of the thumb gusset: k to last 3 sts, m1, k1, m1, k2. Work 3 more rounds. 5th round: k to last 5 sts, m1, k3, m1, k2. Work 3 more rounds. Cont inc, as set, on next and every following 4th row until you have 60 sts, meanwhile placing the graph to correspond with that on the right hand. Work 8 rounds without shaping. **Divide for thumb**: k to last 16 sts, cast on 5 sts, slip next 14 sts onto a thread, k2. Work 14 rounds.

First finger: k first 6 sts of round, slip all but last 8 sts onto a thread, cast on 2 sts, k8 (16 sts). Work as for other hand.

Second finger: k the first 7 sts from the thread, cast on 2 sts, k to last 6 sts, knit up 2 sts from first finger (17 sts). Work as for other hand.

Third finger: k next 6 sts from the thread, cast on 2 sts, k to last 6 sts, knit up 2 sts from the second finger (16 sts). Work as for other hand.

Fourth finger: k remaining 12 sts, knit up 2 sts from third finger (14 sts). Work as for other hand.

DONALD DUCK TODDLERS' SAILOR SUIT

Materials

Melinda Coss mercerized 4-ply cotton – sweater: blue: 150/175gm; red and yellow: less than 25gm of each colour.
Hat: blue: 50gm; black: less than 25gm.
4 large "brass" buttons; approx 80cm of black ribbon, 1.5cm wide.

Needles

One pair 2¾mm and one pair of 3¼mm needles.

Tension

Using 3¼mm needles and measured over st st: 28 sts and 36 rows = 10cm square.

A replica of Donald Duck's sailor sweater and hat for toddlers. Worked in mercerized 4-ply cotton, the sweater instructions are given for 18/24 months; the hat is one sized.

SWEATER

Back

Using 2¾mm needles and base colour, cast on 86/94 sts and work in garter st (knit every row) for 9 rows. Change to 3¼mm needles and cont in st st until work measures 32/37cm. Leave sts on a spare needle.

Front

As for back until work measures 25/30cm.
Divide for neck: work 43/47 sts, turn work and leaving remaining sts on a holder. Dec 1 st at neck edge on every row until 22/24 sts remain. Work straight until it matches the back. Leave sts on a holder and return to other side of neck, joining yarn in at neck edge and shaping to match the first side. Leave sts on a holder.

Sleeves

Using 2¾mm needles and base colour, cast on 42/48 sts and work in garter st, inc 1 st each end of the 3rd/6th row and every following 3rd row.

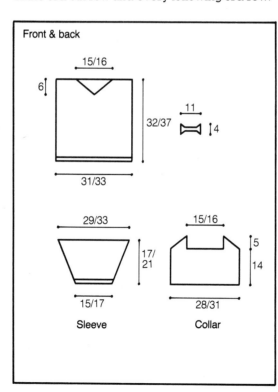

Front & back
15/16
6
32/37
31/33
11
4

29/33
17/21
15/17
Sleeve

15/16
5
14
28/31
Collar

When 8 garter st rows have been worked, change to 3¼mm needles and yellow and work in st st for 9 rows (cont to inc as before). Change back to base colour and cont in st st, inc as before until you have 82/94 sts. Work straight until sleeve measures 17/21cm. Cast off loosely.

Collar

Using 2¾mm needles and yellow, cast on 78/86 sts and work in garter st for 10 rows. Change to 3¼mm needles.
Next (RS) row: k7 yellow, join in base colour, k64/72, join in a second ball of yellow and k7.
Row 2: k7 yellow, p64/72 base colour, k7 yellow. Rep these last 2 rows until the collar measures 14cm, ending with a WS row.
Next row: k7 yellow, k11/13 base colour, cast off 42/46 sts, k11/13 in base, k7 yellow. Cont with this set of sts, putting the other set onto a holder. Work 6/8 rows straight with the yellow border in garter st, as set.
Next (WS) row: k7 yellow, change to base colour, p2 tog, p to end. Row 2: k to last 9 sts, k2 tog, change to yellow and k7. Keep rep the last 2 rows until all base colour sts have been decreased. Cont working the yellow border in garter st, keeping the neck edge straight, while dec 1 st at the outer edge on every row until all sts have been disposed of. Return to the other side of the collar, join in yarn at neck edge and work as for the first side, reversing out shapings.

Bow

Using 3¼mm needles and red, cast on 14 sts and work in garter st, dec 1 st each end of every 3rd row until 6 sts remain. Work straight for 6cm and then inc 1 st each end of every 3rd row until you have 14 sts once again. Cast off.

Making up

Knit one shoulder seam tog (see Techniques, pages 13-14), cast off the 42/46 back neck sts and then cont to knit tog the other shoulder seam. Open out the body and pin sleeves into position, taking care not to bunch them. Join with a narrow backstitch. Join side and sleeve seams with a flat seam over the garter st and a narrow backstitch over the st st. Attach the collar with a flat seam so that the tips of its points just meet at the bottom of the neck V. Tie

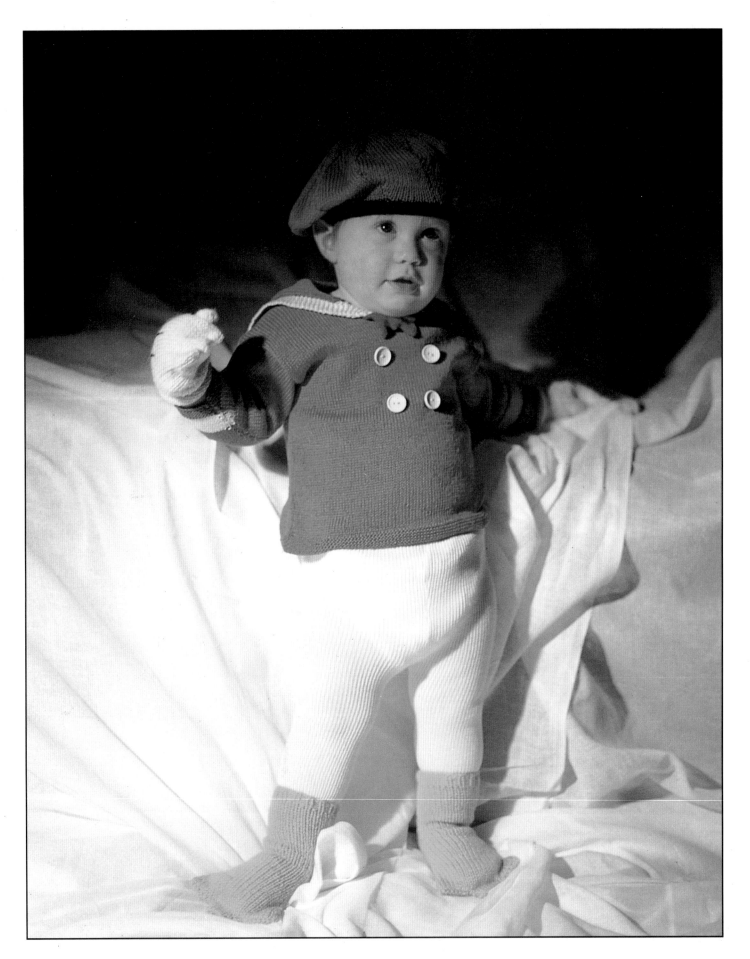

the bow into a single knot in its centre – i.e., the part that was knitted straight – to form a mock bow tie. Stitch this directly at the front of the neck, taking a few sts through the knot so that it will remain knotted. Attach the four buttons to the front, positioning them as in the photograph.

HAT

Using 3¼mm needles and black, cast on 80 sts. Row 1: * k1, p1, rep from * to end. Keep rep this row to form single rib. Work 6 rows in all and then change to blue. Next row: knit, inc into every 8th st. Row 2: purl. Row 3: knit, inc into every 9th st. Cont as set, inc 10 sts every knit row until you have 180 sts. Work 5 rows without shaping.

Next row: *k16, k2 tog, rep from * to end. Row 2: purl. Row 3: *k15, k2 tog, rep from * to end. Cont as set, dec 10 sts every knit row until 10 sts remain.

Next row: p2 tog all along the row. Now draw the yarn up through the remaining sts and secure.

Making up

Sew tog with a flat seam. Take the ribbon, fold it in half and attach it to the top edge of the ribbing at the seam point, as shown. Cut Vs out of the ribbon ends to finish.

MICKEY MOUSE TODDLERS' SUIT

The instructions for these cotton 4-ply shorts and a long-sleeved T-shirt for little Mickeys are given for 18/24 months.

T-SHIRT

Back
Using black and 2¾mm needles, cast on 76/82 sts.
Row 1: *k1, p1, rep from * to end. Keep rep this row to form single rib for 4cm, ending with a WS row. Next row: knit, inc into every 12th/13th st (82/88 sts). Now change to 3¼mm needles and cont in st st, until work measures 19/22cm.
Shape armholes: cast off 3/4 sts at beg of next 2 rows. Now dec 1 st each end of every row until 70/72 sts remain. Work straight until the back measures 31/36 cm, ending with a WS row.
Shape neck and shoulders (*see* Techniques, page 8): k17/18, put these sts on a holder, cast off 36, work to last 5/6 sts, turn and p to last 2 sts, p2 tog. Next row: k2 tog, k to last 10/11 sts, turn work and p to end. Put these sts on a holder and return to the other side of neck. Join yarn in at neck edge and work to match the first side, reversing out the shapings.

Front
As for back until the work measures 28/31cm, ending with a WS row. **Shape neck**: k25/26 sts, cast off 20 sts, work to end. Cont with this set of sts, leaving others on a holder. Dec 1 st at neck edge on every row until 15/16 sts remain. Now work straight, until the front measures 31/37cm, ending with a WS row. **Shape shoulder**: next row: k to last 5/6 sts, turn and p to end.
Row 3: k to last 10/11 sts, turn and p to end. Leave sts on a holder. Return to other side of neck, join yarn in at neck edge and work to match the first side, reversing out shapings. Leave sts on a spare needle.

Sleeves
Using 2¾mm needles cast on 42/48 sts and work in single rib for 4cm. Change to 3¼mm needles and cont in st st, inc 1 st each end of every 4th row until you have 70/76 sts. Work straight until the sleeve measures 22/26cm.
Shape sleeve head: cast off 3/4 sts at beg of next 2 rows. Now dec 1 st each end of every row until 60 sts remain. Cast off 10 sts at beg of next 4 rows. Cast off remaining sts.

Neckband
Knit the left shoulder seam tog (*see* Techniques, pages 13-14). Using 2¾mm needles and with RS of work facing, knit up 42 sts across the back of the neck, 16 sts down the left side of neck, 20 sts across the front and 16 sts up other side of neck (94 sts). Purl the first row and then cont in single rib until the band measures 2.5cm. Cast off loosely in rib.

Making up
Knit the second shoulder seam tog and join the neckband with a flat seam. Join the side and sleeve seams with a flat seam over the ribs, a narrow backstitch over the st st. Set the sleeves into the armholes, distributing the fabric evenly. Pin, and sew with a narrow backstitch.

SHORTS

Back
Start at the lower edge of the left leg. Using 3mm needles and base colour, cast on 46/50 sts.
Row 1: *k1, p1, rep from * to end. Keep rep this row to form single rib for 2cm. Now change to 3¼mm needles and cont in st st, inc 1 st each end of the first row. When work measures 9/10cm, ending with a WS row, **shape crotch**: next row: cast off 3 sts, work to end. Row 2: purl. **Row 3: k1, k2 tog, k to end.** Rep last 2 rows (43/47) sts. Leave these sts on a spare needle. Work the right leg to match, reversing out the shapings and dec by k2 tog through backs of loops (tbl). Now slip the left leg sts onto the same needle, crotch shapings to the centre of the row.
Next row (WS): purl. Row 2: k40/44, k2 tog tbl, k2, k2 tog, k to end (84/92 sts).
Work straight until work measures 25/27cm.
Shape waist: Next row: work to last 10 sts, turn and repeat. 3rd row: work to last 20 sts, turn and repeat. 5th row: work to last 30 sts, turn and repeat. Break off yarn and slip all sts onto the same needle. Now work across all sts dec 1 st in every 10 sts (76/83 sts). Cont in st st for a further 16 rows. Cast off.

Front
Work right leg as for back left leg until work measures 9/10cm, ending with a RS row.
Next row: purl. Row 2: work from ** to ** as for

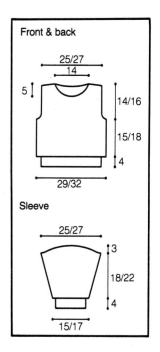

Materials
Shorts: 100/150gm Melinda Coss 4 ply. Top: 150/200gm Melinda Coss 4 ply.
2 large black buttons; 2cm wide ribbon elastic for the shorts.

Needles
One pair 2¾mm, one pair 3mm and one pair 3¼mm needles.

Tension
Using 3¼mm needles and measured over st st: 28 sts and 36 rows = 10cm square.

Front & back

25/27
14

5

14/16

15/18

4

29/32

Sleeve

25/27

3

18/22

4

15/17

the back. Rep these last 2 rows another 2 times more (45/49 sts). Leave these sts on a spare needle and work a left leg to match, reversing out the shapings and knitting 2 tog tbl. Cont as for back, but omitting the turned rows.

Making up

Join seams with a flat seam, leaving the waist seam open for 2cm at the very top on one side. Turn in the cast off edge and slip st it down inside the waist to form a tube 2cm deep. Thread ribbon elastic through the opening which has been left and join its ends according to waist size. Position the buttons as shown in the photograph.

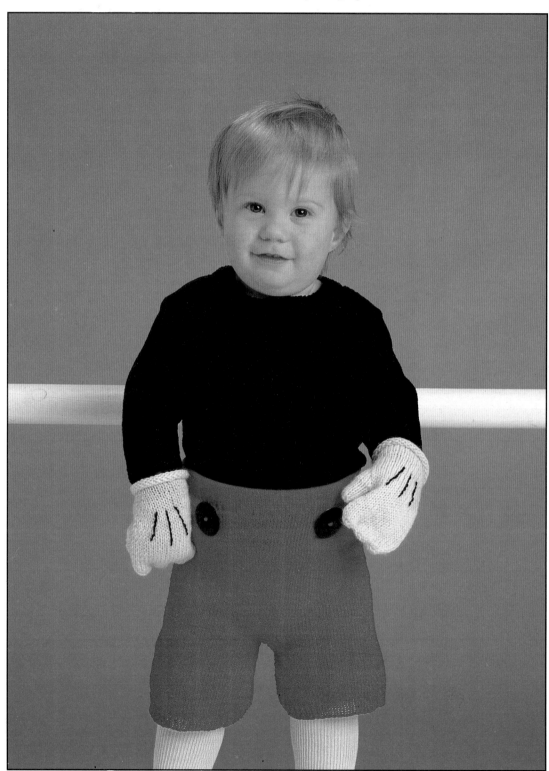

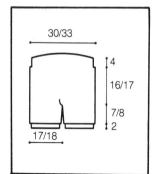

DONALD DUCK TODDLERS' FLIPPERS AND MICKEY MOUSE MITTENS

To complete the character outfits, here are Donald's flippers in sock form and Mickey's three-fingered gloves in mitten form. Both are worked in double knitting wool. The two sizes are for 18/24 months.

FLIPPERS

(Both identical)
Using a set of 3¼mm needles and yellow, cast on 28/32 sts. Place a marker on the needle at the beginning and work in rounds of k1, p1, rib for 2cm. Change to a set of 4mm needles and cont in st st until the sock measures 7/9cm.
Divide for heel: halve the sts, leaving the back 14/16 sts (with the marker in the centre) on one needle and putting the instep sts on a thread to hold them. **Turn the heel**: keeping in st st, work back and forth on the heel sts, leaving an additional one unworked at the end of every row (*see* Techniques, page 8), until only 4 sts are being worked.
Cont to work in rounds again, placing the instep sts back on the needles. Work straight for 4cm from last turned row. Place 2 more markers 6/8 sts either side of the central marker, which should now be removed. On the next round, inc 1 st (by working into the st on the row below the next st and then working the st itself) from the st after the first marker and inc another from the st before the 2nd marker. Cont inc 1 st at each of these positions on every alt round until you have 44/48 sts on the needles (6/8 inc either side). Complete the round (to the point where the central marker had been). Next row: k5, cast off 12/14, k10 and leave these holding on one of the needles. Cast off 12/14, k to end of round and then 5 sts from the next round. Cont with these 10 sts on 2 needles. Row 2: p2 tog, p to last 2 sts, p2 tog tbl. Knit the next row and then rep row 2. Work 0/1 row. Cast off. Return to the other 10 sts being held and work to match.

Making up
Join the toe ends with a flat seam.

MITTENS

Left hand
Using a pair of 4mm needles and natural, cast on 26/28 sts and work in st st for 3cm, ending with a WS row.
Next row: k1, inc 1 (work into the st on the row below the next one to be worked and then the st itself), k to last 2 sts, inc 1, k1. Work 3 rows straight and then rep inc row. Work 1 row straight.
Shape thumb gusset: Next row: k14/15, inc 1, k to end. Row 2 (and all WS rows): purl. Row 3: k1, inc 1, k12/13, inc 1 twice, k to last 2 sts, inc 1, k1. Row 5: k1, inc 1, k13/14, inc 1, k2, inc 1, k to last 2 sts, inc 1, k1 (39/41 sts). Now work the sides straight but cont to shape thumb gusset. Row 7: k16/17, inc 1, k4, inc 1, k to end. Row 9: k16/17, inc 1, k6, inc 1, k to end. Cont as set until you have 43/47 sts on the needle.
Next RS row: k16/17, slip the next 9/11 sts onto a thread, k to end, making sure that there is no stretched strand bridging the gap formed by the held sts. Work straight until the mitten measures 11/12cm, ending with a RS row.
Shape top: p16/17, sl 1, p2 tog, psso. Row 2: k1, sl 1, k1, psso, k to last 2 sts, k2 tog. Row 3: p14/15, sl 1, p2 tog, psso, p to end. Row 4: rep row 2. Cast off tightly.
Work thumb: return to held sts and put them onto the set of double-pointed 4mm needles, inc 1 st from the base of the thumb. Work in rounds until it measures 3cm from the first round. K2 tog all around next row and then draw yarn through remaining sts and secure.

Right hand
As for left hand but reversing the thumb gusset so that the first inc row reads: k16/17, inc 1, k to end.

Making up
Join side and tops with a flat seam. On the RS, divide the tops into three and using natural yarn work a few very tight oversewn sts at the 2 points to create a slight indentation to give the impression of three fingers. Using black yarn, embroider the 3 black lines, as shown, using a small backstitch.

Materials
Flippers: 50gm of yellow Melinda Coss DK wool.
Mittens: 50gm of natural Melinda Coss DK wool plus a small length of black wool for embroidery.

Needles
One pair of 4mm needles, a set of double-pointed 4mm needles and a set of double-pointed 3¼mm needles.

Tension
Using 4mm needles and measured over st st: 24 sts and 32 rows = 10cm square.

DUMBO TODDLERS' OUTFIT

A skirt suit with a raglan top for 2/3 year olds and a trouser suit with a drop-shoulder top to fit 1 year olds. Both incorporate the Dumbo motif, and the trouser suit is accompanied by Dumbo's hat and a striped scarf.

SKIRT

Knitted in one piece with a seam up the back.
Using 2¾mm needles and base colour, cast on 180 sts.
Row 1:*k2, p2, rep from * to end. Keep rep this

Materials

Melinda Coss 4-ply wool –
base colour: raglan
sweater: 200gm; skirt:
125gm; drop-shoulder
sweater: 150gm; trousers:
150gm; hat: 50gm; scarf:
100gm; contrasts: less than
25gm of each colour,
matched exactly to the
graph.
Both the skirt and trousers
require ribbon elastic,
2.5cm wide, length
according to waist size. The
drop-shoulder sweater
requires 3 buttons.

Needles

One pair each of 3¼mm,
3mm and 2¾mm needles; a
set of double-pointed
2¾mm and a set of double-
pointed 3¼mm needles for
the raglan sweater collar
and the hat.

Tension

Using 3¼mm needles and
measured over st st: 28 sts
and 36 rows = 10cm
square.
N.B. Make every effort to
keep your tension the same
when working the colour
motif. Do not carry the base
colour behind the colour
motif.

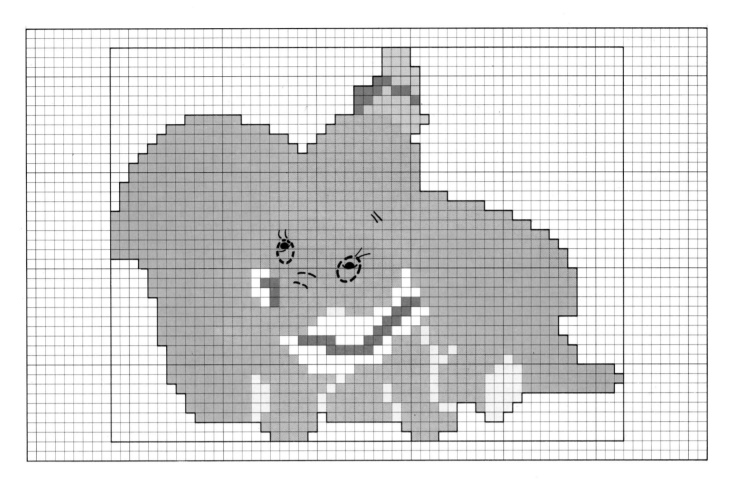

row to form double rib until the work measures 4cm, ending with a WS row.

Next row: k, inc into every 22nd st (188 sts). Change to 3¼mm needles, purl the next row and cont in st st until the work measures 9cm, ending on a WS row. Next row: k51, work first row of graph, k to end. Cont working the graph in this position until it is complete. Now cont in base colour until work measures 39cm. Cast off.

Making up

Sew the back seam with a flat seam, leaving 2.5cm open at the top. Turn this depth in to form the waistband and slip st down. Thread ribbon elastic through the waistband tube and join, end across end, according to waist size. Embroider Dumbo's eyes as illustrated (*see* Techniques, page 16).

RAGLAN SWEATER

Back

Using 2¾mm needles and base colour, cast on 90 sts and work in double rib for 2.5cm, ending on a WS row.

Next row: k, inc into every 22nd st (94 sts). Change to 3¼mm needles, purl the next row and cont in st st until work measures 16cm.

Shape raglan: cast off 4 sts at beg of next 2 rows. Dec 1 each end of the next and every

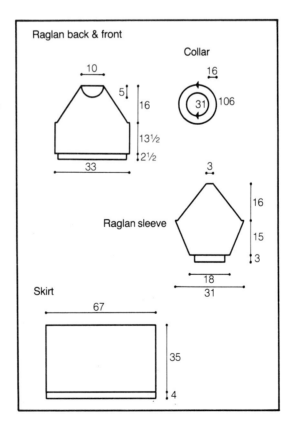

following alt row until 28 sts remain. Work 1 row straight. Leave sts on a holder.

Front

As for back until 46 sts remain. Next row **shape neck**: work 16 sts, put remaining sts on a holder and turn work. Now dec 1 st each end of every alt row until 3 sts remain. Work 1 row straight. Dec 1 st at raglan edge on next row. Work 1 row straight. Work 2 tog and pull yarn through final st to secure. Return to the other side of the neck, leaving the central 14 sts on the holder. Shape to match first side.

Sleeves

Using 2¾mm needles and base colour, cast on 44 sts and work in k2, p2 rib for 3cm.
Next RS row: k, inc into every 7th st (50 sts). Change to 3¼mm needles, purl the next row and cont in st st, inc 1 st each end of the next and every following 3rd row until you have 82 sts. Now inc 1 st each end of every alt row until you have 88 sts. Work 2 rows straight. **Shape raglan**: cast off 4 sts at beg of next 2 rows and then dec 1 st each end of every alt row until you have 30 sts. Now dec 1 st each end of every row until you have 10 sts. Leave sts on a holder.

Collar

Join the raglan seams with a very narrow backstitch. Using a set of double-pointed 2¾mm needles, base colour and with the RS of work facing, knit up 13 sts down the left side of neck, knit the 14 centre sts onto a needle, knit up 13 sts up the right side of neck and then knit the right sleeve, back neck and left sleeve sts onto a needle (88 sts). Work in k1, p1 rib for 2.5cm. Change to a set of 3¼mm needles and work in st st, remembering that the RS must be on the collar when it is turned back, as in the photograph.
Row 2: *k1 (knit into the st below the next one on the left-hand needle and then into the st itself) known as inc 1, rep from * to end of row (132 sts). Work 1 more row and then repeat the inc row (198 sts). Work 1 more row and then repeat the increase row once again (297 sts). Cont in st st until work measures 10cm from the last row of rib, ending with a WS row. Now change to red and work 4 rows. Change back to base colour. Work 2 more rows in st st. Change to 2¾mm needles and work 6 rows in garter st (since you are working in the round this must be worked as purl 1 row, knit 1 row). Cast off loosely, using a 3¼mm needle.

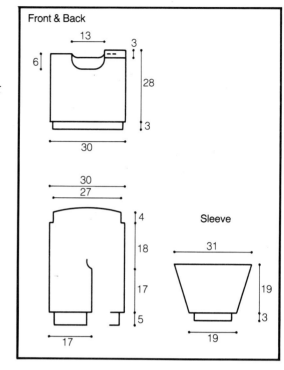

Front & Back
13
3
6
28
3
30

30
27
4
18
17
5
17

Sleeve
31
19
3
19

Making up

Sew the side and sleeve seams with a flat seam on the ribs, a narrow backstitch on the remainder.

TROUSERS

Back

Start at the lower edge of the left leg. Using 2¾mm needles and base colour, cast on 36 sts.
Row 1: *k1, p1, rep from * to end. Keep rep this row to form single rib for 5cm, ending with a WS row. Knit the next row, inc into every 3rd st (48 sts). Change to 3¼mm needles and cont in st st until work measures 22cm, ending with a WS row. **Shape crotch**: next row: cast off 3 sts, work to end. Row 2: purl. Row 3: **k1, k2 tog, k to end.** Rep last 2 rows (43 sts). Leave these sts on a spare needle.
Work the right leg to match, reversing out the shapings and dec by k2 tog tbl. Now slip the left leg sts onto the same needle, crotch shapings to the centre of the row. Next row (WS): purl. Row 2: k40, k2 tog tbl, k2, k2 tog, k to end (84 sts). Work straight until work measures 40cm.
Shape waist: Next row: work to last 10 sts, turn and repeat. 3rd row: work to last 20 sts, turn and repeat. 5th row: work to last 30 sts, turn and repeat. Break off yarn and slip all sts onto the same needle. Now work across all sts dec 1 st every 10th st (76 sts). Cont in st st for a further 16 rows. Cast off.

Front

Work right leg as for back left leg until work measures 22cm, ending with a RS row. Next row: purl. Row 2: work from ** to ** as for the back. Rep these last 2 rows twice more (45 sts). Leave these sts on a spare needle and work a left leg to match, reversing out the shapings and knitting 2 tog tbl. Cont as for back, but omitting the turned rows.

Making up

Join seams with a flat seam, leaving the waist seam open for 2.5cm at the top on one side. Turn in the cast off edge and slip st it down inside the waist to form a tube 2.5cm deep. Thread ribbon elastic through the opening which has been left and join it, end over end, according to waist size.

DROP-SHOULDER SWEATER

Back

Using 3mm needles and base colour, cast on 85 sts and work in k1, p1 rib for 3cm. Change to 3¼mm needles and cont in st st until work measures 28.5cm. **Shape neck**: next RS row

k26, cast off 33, k to end. Cont with this set of sts, leaving the others on a holder. Dec 1 st at neck edge on next two alt rows. Change to 3mm needles and work remaining 24 sts in k1, p1 rib for 12 rows. Cast off in rib. Return to held sts, shape as for first side of neck and then cont straight in st st until work measures 31cm from the beg. Leave sts on a spare needle.

Front

As for back until work measures 10cm, ending with a WS row.
Next row: k15, knit the first row of graph, k to end. Cont working the graph in this position until it is completed. Now cont in base colour until work measures 25cm, ending with a WS row.
Shape neck: work 34, cast off 17, work to end. Cont with this set of sts, dec 1 st at neck edge on every row until 24 sts remain. Work straight until it measures 31cm from the beg. Leave sts on a holder. Return to the other set of sts, and shape to match first side of neck. Now work straight until it measures 29.5cm from beg. Change to 3mm needles and cont in k1, p1 rib for 8 rows. On the next row **form buttonholes**: *rib 7 sts, cast off 1 st, rep from * once more and then rib to end. Rib next row, casting on 1 st above each st cast off on the previous row. Rib 2 more rows. Cast off in rib.

Neckband

Knit tog the left shoulder seam from armhole to neck (see Techniques, pages 13-14). Using a 2¾mm needle and with RS of work facing you, knit up 20 sts down the left side of the neck (starting at the top edge of buttonhole band), 17 sts across the front, 16 sts up the other side of the neck and 49 sts across the back neck, finishing at the edge of the buttonband (102 sts). Using 3mm needles, purl the first row and then rib 6 rows.
On the next row form a buttonhole: rib 2, cast off 1 st, rib to end. Rib the next row, casting on a st directly above that cast off on the previous row. Rib 3 more rows and then cast off loosely, in rib.

Sleeves

Using 2¾mm needles and base colour, cast on 48 sts and work in k1, p1 rib for 3cm, ending with a WS. Next row: knit, inc into every 9th st (53 sts). Change to 3¼mm needles and cont in st st, inc 1 st each end of every 4th row until you have 87 sts. Work 1 row straight and then cast off loosely.

Making up

Open out the body and pin the sleeves, avoiding bunching them. On the buttonband side, overlap the ribs before attaching the sleeve. Stitch with a narrow backstitch. Join side and sleeve seams with a flat seam on the ribs and a narrow backstitch for the st st. Attach buttons to correspond with buttonholes. Embroider Dumbo's eyes, as illustrated (see Techniques, page 16).

SCARF

Using 3¼mm needles and white, cast on 58 sts.
Row 1: white *k1, p1, rep from * 5 more times, put yarn to back of work and join in red, twisting the strands to avoid a gap, (see Techniques, page 10), red **k1, p1, rep from ** twice more, put yarn to back of work and join in a second ball of white, twisting the strands as before. Rib to end.
Row 2: Rib in colours as set but twisting the yarns at the front of the work each time the colour changes. Cont in rib, using three separate balls of yarn until work measures 70cm, ending on a WS row. Now cast off knitwise, using the first ball of base colour yarn all the way across.
Finish off by attaching fringes of white yarn along cast on and cast off edges (see Techniques, page 16).

HAT

Using double-pointed, 2¾mm needles and blue, cast on 116 sts and work in st st rounds for 14cm. Now work in single rib for 2.5cm. Change to a set of 3¼mm needles and cont in st st, for 5cm more, reversing the RS since the first band of st st is to be turned back on itself. Divide the sts exactly into 4 and place a marker at every 29th st. These 4 sts are the axial sts. Dec 1 st each side of every axial st on the next and every following 4th row until 12 sts remain. K2 tog all the way across the next round. Thread the yarn through the remaining sts, pull it tight and secure on the inside of the hat.

Making up

Fold the band of st st in half, back on itself, so that the RS is facing and loosely slip st down around the first row of the ribbing. Lightly press the fold into position.

FILMSTRIP FAIRISLE SWEATER

A drop-shoulder sweater for men and women in 4-ply wool featuring Mickey and Minnie on celluloid and with a choice of V- or round-necks. The fairisle technique of colour knitting is used throughout (*see* Techniques, page 9) and the instructions are given women's/men's (see diagrams for actual measurements).

Back

Using 2¾mm needles and base colour, cast on 150 sts.

Row 1: *k1, p1, rep from * to end. Keep rep to form single rib for 6cm, ending on a RS row. Purl the next row, inc into the first 2 and last 2 sts of the row (154 sts). Change to 3¼mm needles and start working from graphs, keeping in st st throughout. Work the border graph and then 2 rows in base colour only.

Graph 1: k1 in base colour, k first row of graph working 4 repeats in all, k1 in base colour. Work as set until the 27 rows are complete. *Now work 3 rows in base, followed by another border and then 2/4 rows in base.*

Graph 2: k4 in base colour, k first row of graph working 10 repeats in all. Work as set until the 29 rows are complete. Now work from * to *.

Graph 3: k4 in base colour, k first row of graph, working 5 repeats in all. Work as set until the 28 rows are complete. **Now work 2/4 rows in base, followed by another border and then 2/4 rows in base.**

Graph 4: as for graph 3. Work from ** to **. Leave sts on a spare needle.

Front for V-neck version

Women's: as for back until 13 rows of graph 3 have been worked. Men's: as for back until graph 3 is completed. Finish with 2/4 base colour rows.

Divide for neck (meanwhile cont in pattern as for back): pattern 77 sts and turn work, leaving remaining sts on a holder. Cont with this set of sts, dec 1 st at neck edge on every row for 3 rows. Now dec 1 st at this edge on every alt row until 53/52 sts remain. Work straight until the pattern has been completed, as on back. Leave sts on a holder. Return to the other side of the neck, join in yarn at neck edge and shape to match the first side. Leave sts on a holder.

Front for round-neck version

Work as for back until 16 rows of graph 4 have been worked.

Row 17: work 66 sts, cast off 22 sts, work to end. Cont with this set of sts, keeping in pattern throughout, leaving others on a holder. Dec 1 st at neck edge on every row until 46 sts remain. Now work straight until the front matches the back. Leave sts on a holder. Return to other set of sts, join in yarn at neck edge and shape to match first side. Leave sts on a holder.

Sleeves

Using 2¾mm needles and base colour, cast on 56 sts and work in single rib for 8/10cm, ending with a RS row. Next row: purl, inc into every 3rd st (74 sts). Now change to 3¼mm needles and start working the graphs and base colour rows in exactly the same sequence as on the back, working as many st repeats or part repeats as will fit the number of sts. Meanwhile inc 1 st each end of every 4th row until you have 124 sts (working all new sts into colour pattern as you go). Now inc 1 st each end of every 3rd row until there are 132/140 sts. Work straight until the border that follows graph 3 is complete. Cast off loosely.

Materials

Melinda Coss 4-ply wool – base colour: 500/550gm; black: 100/100gm; red: 75/75gm; yellow: 50/50gm; white 75/75gm.

Needles

One pair of 2¾mm and one pair of 3¼mm needles.

Tension

Using 3¼mm needles and measured over colour pattern not base colour st st: 28 sts and 28 rows = 10cm square.

Front & back

Sleeve

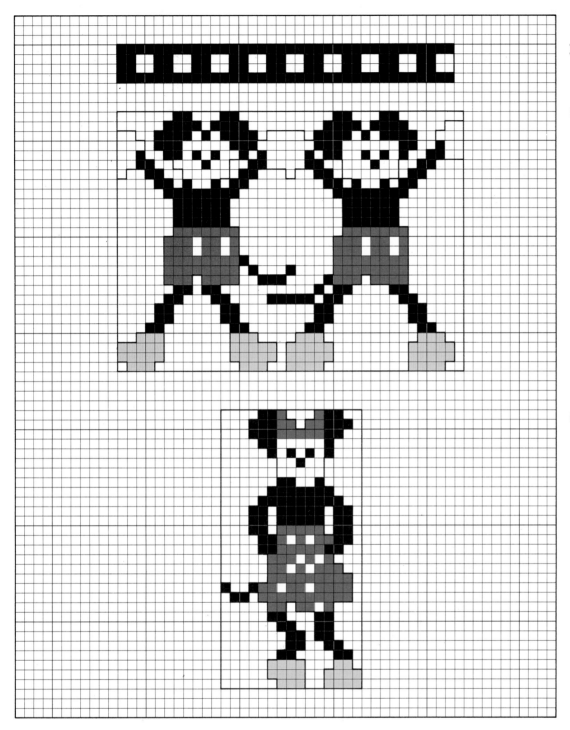

Border graph

Graph 1

Graph 2

V neckband

Knit the left shoulder seam together from armhole to neck edge (*see* Techniques, pages 13-14). Using 2¾mm needles, slip the 48/50 back neck sts on to one needle and then with the RS facing, knit up 64/66 sts down the left side of neck, 1 st from the strand where the neck was divided (this becoming the axial st), and 64/66 sts up the other side (177/183 sts). Purl the first row.

Next row: *k1, p1, keep rep from * to 2 sts

before the axial st, k2 tog, k the axial st, k2 tog, **p1, k1, keep rep from ** to end.
Row 2: rib to 2 sts before axial st, k2 tog, p the axial st, k2 tog, **p1, k1, keep rep from ** to end. Rep the last 2 rows until the border is 3cm deep. Cast off in rib.

Round neckband

Knit the left shoulder seam tog. Using 2¾mm needles, slip the 62 back neck sts on to one needle and then with RS facing, knit up 18 sts

Graph 3

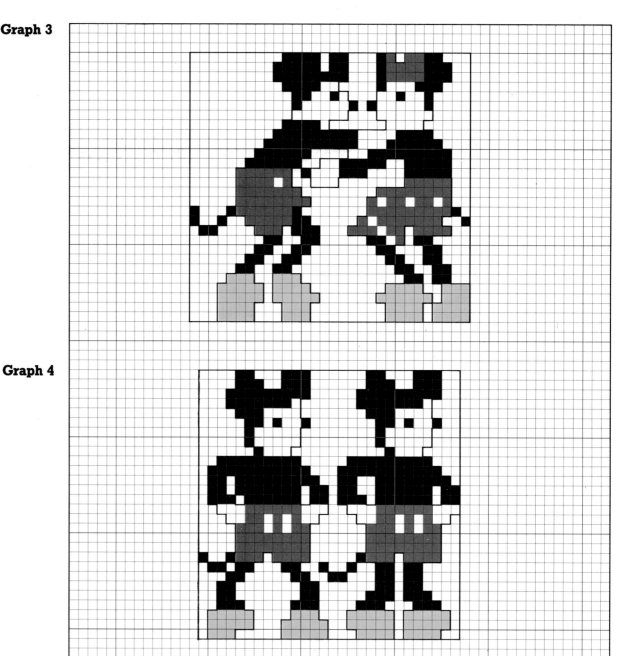

Graph 4

down the left side of the neck, 22 across the front and 18 up the other side (120 sts). Purl the first row and then work in single rib for 3cm. Cast off loosely in rib.

Making up
Knit right shoulder seam tog and join neckband with a flat seam. Open out the body and pin the sleeves in position, taking care that they are not bunched or stretched. Attach with backstitch. Join all other seams with a flat seam across the ribs and backstitch over the st st.

GOOFY JACKET

An oversized, chunky-weight jacket with a shawl neck and zip fastening. A giant Goofy motif is featured on the back panel, the red of his shirt being echoed in the stripe borders of all five pockets. With its drop shoulders and deep cuffs, this one-size jacket is suitable for men or women.

Materials
Melinda Coss chunky wool – blue: 1600gm; black: 150gm; red: 200gm; yellow: 100gm; white: 200gm. One 73cm open-ended zip fastener.

Needles
One pair of 6½mm and one pair of 5½mm needles.

Tension
Using 6½mm needles and measured over st st: 14 sts and 19 rows = 10cm square.
N.B. Make every effort to keep your tension the same when working the colour motif. Do not carry the base colour behind the motif.

Pocket linings

Worked in st st on 6½mm needles using blue. Leave each one on a spare needle until required.

For fronts (work 2): cast on 31 sts and work for 16cm.

For breast pocket: cast on 25 sts and work for 14cm.

For sleeves (work 2): cast on 29 sts and work for 15cm.

Back

Using 5½mm needles and blue, cast on 92 sts. Row 1: * k2, p2, rep from * to end. Keep rep this row to form double rib until it measures 7cm, ending with a WS row.

Change to 6½mm needles and cont in st st, working the graph thus: row 1: k7, k the first row of the graph, k to end. Cont working the graph in this position until it is complete. Work 6 rows in base colour only. Leave sts on a holder.

Right front

Using 5½mm needles and blue, cast on 48 sts. Row 1: k4, * p2, k2, rep from * to end. Row 2: * p2, k2, rep from * to last 4 sts, k4. Cont thus, in double rib with a 4 st garter st border, until the work measures 7cm, ending with a WS row.

Change to 6½mm needles. Now cont in st st, except for the 4 border sts, which are cont in garter st throughout. When work measures

28cm, ending on a WS row, **work pocket**: k8, slip the next 31 sts onto a holder and work the 31 pocket lining sts instead, k to end of row. Cont as before until the work measures 63cm, ending with a WS row. **Work breast pocket**: k8, slip the next 25 sts onto a holder and work the 25 pocket lining sts instead, k to end of row. Cont as before until work measures 73cm, ending on a WS row. **Shape neck**: cast off 7 sts, k to end. Now dec 1 st at neck edge on every row until 36 sts remain. Now dec 1 st at neck edge on every alt row until 33 sts remain. Work straight until front matches back. Leave sts on a spare needle.

Left front

As for right front, reversing out shapings and omitting the breast pocket.

Sleeves

Using 5½mm needles and blue, cast on 40 sts and work in double rib for 4 rows. Change to red and rib 2 rows. Change back to blue and cont in rib until work measures 15cm. Change to 6½mm needles and cont in st st, inc 1 st each end of next and every following 4th row until you have 68 sts. Next RS row **work pocket**: k19, slip the next 29 sts onto a holder and work the pocket linings sts instead, k to end. Cont shaping sleeve as before until you have 82 sts. Work straight until sleeve measures 59cm. Cast off loosely.

Collar

Using 6½mm needles and blue, cast on 8 sts. Knit every row, inc 1 st each end of every alt row, 1 st in from the edge, until you have 16 sts. Now work 1 edge straight while inc 1 st on every row on the other edge until you have 22 sts. Work straight for 72 rows. Now shape the other end to match, dec instead of inc until 8 sts are left. Cast off.

Pocket borders

Using 5½mm needles and blue, work the held sts above each pocket in k1, p1 rib, starting with a RS row. Rib 2 rows blue, one row red and 1 more row blue. Cast off knitwise, in blue, taking care not to do so too tightly.

Making up

Knit one shoulder seam tog (see Techniques, pages 13-14), cast off the 26 back neck sts and then knit the other shoulder seam tog. Slip stitch the side edges of the pocket borders to the main work, keeping them neat and straight. Pin the zipper into position so that the front

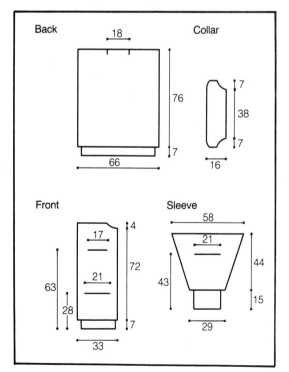

edges of the knitting barely touch one another. Using sewing thread, slip st the inner edges of the zipper to the inside of the knitting, taking care to work strong, firm sts which are not visible on the right side of the work.

Attach the collar to the neckline by its more shaped side, lining up the cast on/off edges of the collar with the cast off edges at the front of the neckline. Use a flat seam.

Open the work out and pin the sleeves to the body, avoiding bunching or stretching them. Attach with a flat seam. Join the side and sleeve seams similarly.

JUNGLE BOOK WOMEN'S SWEATER

A one-size sweater for women with a round neck and drop shoulders. Worked in mohair, it features the *Jungle Book* characters Baloo, King Louis and Kaa.

Materials
Melinda Coss mohair – cream: 100gm; jade: 75gm; emerald, silver, rust and chocolate: 50gm of each; less than 25gm of each of the other colours matched exactly to the graphs.

Needles
One pair of 6mm and one pair of 4½mm needles.

Tension
Using 6mm needles and measured over st st: 16 sts and 16 rows = 10cm square.

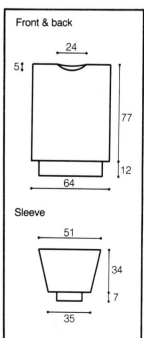

Front & back

24

5↕

77

12

64

Sleeve

51

34

7

35

Back

Using size 4½mm needles and chocolate, cast on 88 sts.

Row 1: *k1, p1, rep from * to end. Keep rep this row to form single rib for 12cm, ending on a RS row. Purl the next row, inc into every 6th st (102 sts).

Change to 6mm needles and work from appropriate graph. Where marked on graph, **shape neck**: work 34 sts, cast off 34 sts, work to end. Cont with this set of sts, leaving others on a holder. Dec 1 st at neck edge on next 3 rows. Leave sts on a holder and return to other side of neck. Join in yarn at neck edge and shape to match first side. Leave sts on a holder.

Front

As for back but working from the appropriate graph. Where marked on graph, **shape neck**: work 39 sts, cast off 24 sts, work to end. Cont with this set of sts, leaving others on a holder. Dec 1 st at neck edge on every row until 32 sts remain. Work 1 row straight. Leave sts on a holder and return to other side of neck. Join yarn in at neck edge and shape to match the first side. Leave sts on a holder.

Left sleeve

Using 4½mm needles and jade, cast on 36 sts and work in single rib for 7cm, ending with a RS row. Purl the next row, inc into every alt st (54 sts). Change to 6mm needles and cont in st

st, working from the graph (page 60) and inc 1 st each end of the first and every following 4th row until you have 82 sts. Work 2 rows straight. Cast off loosely.

Right sleeve

As for left sleeve but work the rib in silver and then work from the graph for the right sleeve (page 60).

Neckband

Knit the left shoulder seam tog (*see* Techniques, pages 13-14). Using 4½mm needles, emerald and with RS facing, knit up 38 sts from around the back neck, 7 sts down the left front, 24 sts across the centre and 7 sts up the other side of neck (76 sts). Purl the first row and then work in single rib for 6cm. Do not cast off but put the sts on to a thread.

Making up

Knit the second shoulder seam tog and join the neckband edges with a flat seam. Turn the neckband in and slip st the held sts down to the point where they were originally picked up around the neckline (*see* Techniques, page 13). Open out the body and pin the sleeves into position, distributing them equally either side of the shoulder seams; avoid bunching them. Join with a flat seam. Join side and sleeve seams likewise.

The top graph on page 60 should be worked into the left sleeve while the lower graph, Kaa, should be incorporated into the right sleeve.

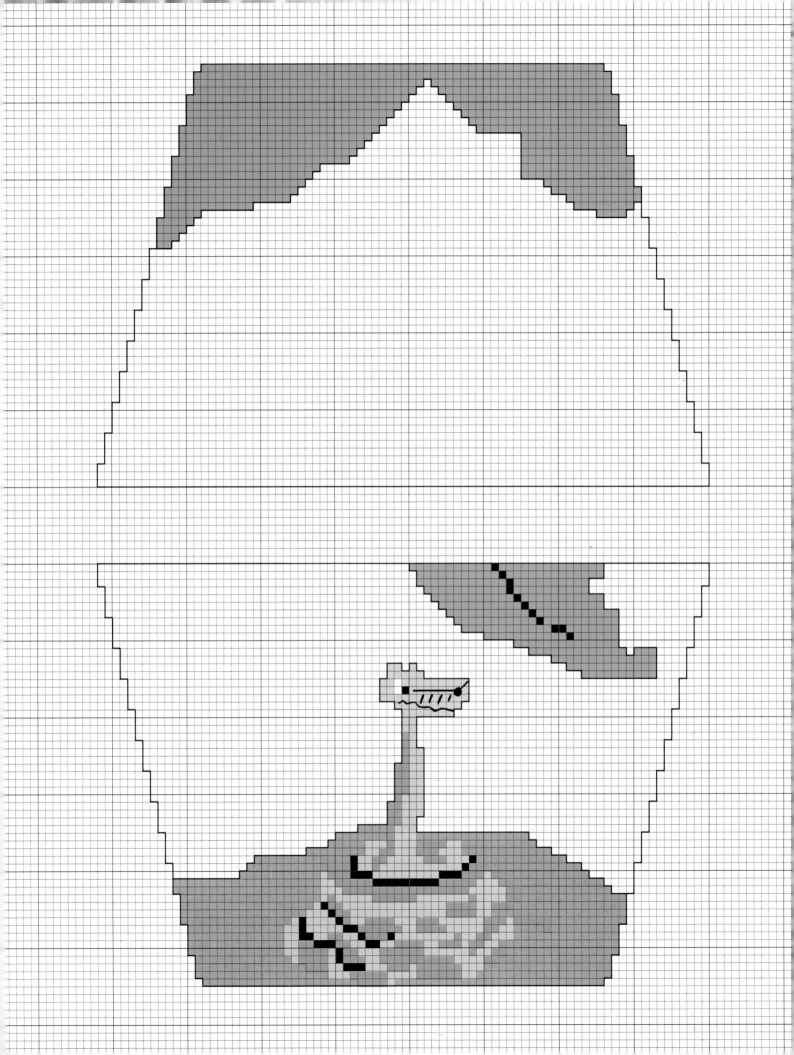

CHUNKY SWEATER FOR KIDS

A basic drop-shoulder, crew-neck sweater for 6/8/10 year olds, worked in chunky-weight wool. There is a choice of four character motifs: Minnie Mouse and Thumper may be worked on any size, but Donald Duck and the White Rabbit are for the two larger sizes only.

Back

Using base colour and 5½mm needles, cast on 48/52/56 sts.

Row 1: *k2, p2, rep from * to end. Keep rep this row to form double rib until it measures 6cm, ending on a RS row. Next row: purl, inc into every 8th/8th/9th st (54/58/62 sts). Change to 6½mm needles and cont in st st until work

Materials

Melinda Coss chunky wool – base colour: size 1 (6 years): 550gm; size 2 (8 years): 600gm; size 3 (10 years): 675gm; contrasts: less than 50gm of each colour, matched exactly to the graphs.

Needles

One pair of 6½mm and one pair of 5½mm needles; a set of double-pointed 5½mm needles.

Tension

Using 6½mm needles and measured over st st: 14 sts and 19 rows = 10cm square. **N.B.** Make every effort to keep your tension the same when working the colour motifs. Do not carry base colours behind the motifs.

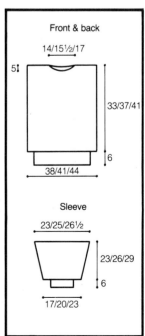

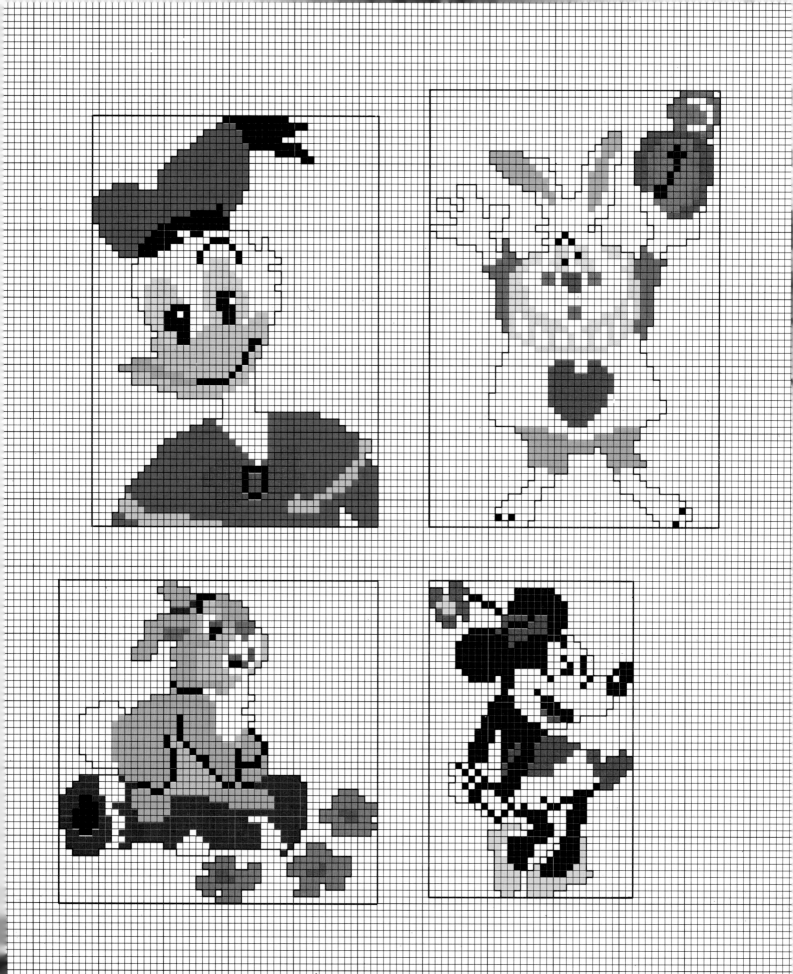

measures 38/42/46cm. **Shape neck**: work 19/20/21 sts, put 16/18/20 sts on a holder, work to end. Now cont working both sides of the neck simultaneously, joining in a second ball of yarn at the first neck edge in order to do so. Dec 1 st at both neck edges on the next two rows. Leave sts on a spare needle.

Front

As for back until the rib is completed and the increase row has been worked.
Row 2: change to 6½mm needles and k0/2/4, work chosen graph sts, k to end. Work graph in this position until it is complete. Now cont in base colour until the work measures 34/38/42cm. Next RS row **shape neck**: work 22/23/24 sts, put 10/12/14 sts on a holder, work to end. Now dec 1 st at both neck edges on every row (working both sides simultaneously as for back), until 17/18/19 shoulder sts remain each side. Now work straight until the front matches the back. Leave sts on a spare needle.

Sleeves

Using 5½mm needles and base colour, cast on 24/28/32 sts and work in double rib for 6cm. Change to 6½mm needles and cont in st st, inc 1 st each end of next 4th/1st/5th row and every following 4th/5th/5th row until you have 44/48/52 sts. Work straight until sleeve measures 29/32/35cm. Cast off loosely.

Neckband

Knit both shoulder seams tog (*see* Techniques, pages 13-14). Using double-pointed 5½mm needles, base colour and with RS of work facing you, knit up 12 sts around the left side of the neck, knit the 10/12/14 front neck sts onto the needle, knit up 12 sts around the right side of the neck and then knit the 16/18/20 back neck sts onto the needle (50/54/58 sts). Work in double rib for 2.5cm. Cast off in rib.

Making up

Open the work out and pin the sleeves to the body, avoiding bunching or stretching them. Attach with a flat seam. Join the neckband, side and sleeve seams with a flat seam.

STARS AND STRIPES MEN'S SWEATER

Materials

Melinda Coss DK cotton –
base colour: 1 kilo; red:
250gm; white: 200gm; pink:
50gm; black: 50gm; silver
ribbon: 100gm.

Needles

One pair of 3¼mm and one
pair of 3¾mm needles.

Tension

Using 3¾mm needles and
measured over st st: 24 sts
and 30 rows = 10cm
square.
N.B. Use intarsia method of
working not fairisle (*see*
Techniques, page 9).

A man-size Mickey Mouse sweater with a slash
neck and drop shoulders worked in crisp cotton
with lurex stars.

Front

Using 3¼mm needles and blue, cast on 120 sts.
Row 1: *k1, p1, rep from * to end. Keep rep this
row to form single rib for 10cm, ending with a
RS row. Next row: purl, inc into first and every
following 7th st (138 sts). Change to 3¾mm
needles and cont in st st, working he 36 rows of
the stars and stripes border. Now change back

to blue and work 4 more rows. Next row: k34, k
the first row of the Mickey graph, k to end.
Cont working the graph in this position until it is
complete. Work 3 more rows in blue only and
then start working the stripe border, omitting
the stars. Work 8 rows. Cont in stripe pattern
but incorporate a single rib neck border thus:
next row: k39, rib 60, k to end. Cont with stripes
but keep the rib in red throughout. When 18
stripe rows have been worked, leave sts on a
holder.

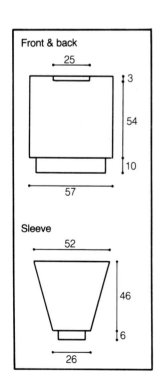

Front & back

25

3

54

10

57

Sleeve

52

46

6

26

Back

As for front, working the stars and stripes bands but omitting the Mickey graph. Work the same number of rows in plain blue.

Sleeves

Using 3¼mm needles and blue, cast on 56 sts and work in single rib for 6cm, ending with a RS row.

Next row: purl, inc into every 9th st (62 sts). Change to 3¾mm needles and cont in st st working the stars and stripes graph, vertically, as a central panel so that the first row reads: blue k13, k first row of graph, blue k to end. Cont with panel centred, inc 1 st each end of every 4th row until there are 126 sts.

Now work straight until 2 rows short of the end of the graph. Cast off firmly but not too tightly, using the relevant colour for each area.

Making up

Knit one shoulder seam together (*see* Techniques, pages 13-14). Cast off the front border ribbed sts and then knit the other shoulder seam tog. Cast off back neck border. Open the work out and pin the sleeves in position, taking great care to line up the stripes (the body stripes may need a light press to ensure that they correspond exactly with the sleeve stripes). Join with a flat seam, then join the side and sleeve seams likewise.

The stars and stripes graph should be worked vertically for the sleeves and horizontally, left to right, on the front and back of the sweater.

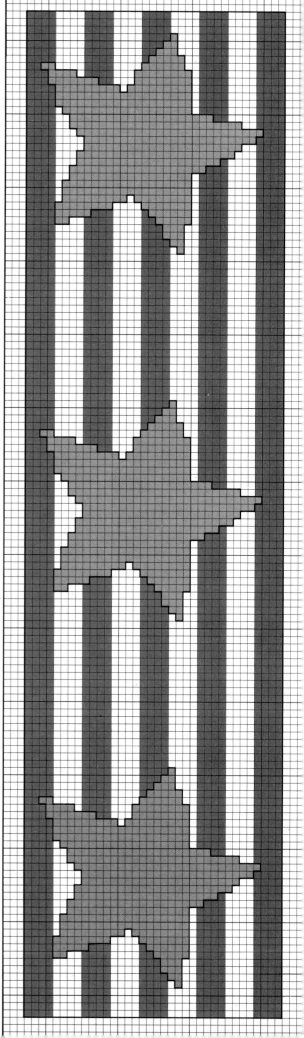

MICKEY MOUSE KIDS' JACKET

A miniature version of the over-sized Goofy jacket shown on page 51. Scaled down for 3/4 year olds, this jacket features Mickey Mouse on the back panel.

Pocket linings
Worked in st st on 6½mm needles using blue. Leave each one on a spare needle until required.
For fronts (work 2): cast on 12 sts and work for 6cm.
For sleeves (work 2): cast on 15 sts and work for 6cm.

Back
Using 5½mm needles and blue, cast on 52 sts. Row 1: *k2, p2, rep from * to end. Keep rep this row to form double rib. Work 2 rows in blue, 2 rows in red and then cont in blue until work measures 6cm, ending with a RS row.
Change to 6½mm needles and purl the next row, inc into every 13th st (56 sts). Next row: k2, k the first row of the graph, k2. Cont working the graph in this position until it is complete. Now cont in base colour only until work measures 44cm, ending with a WS row.
Shape neck and shoulders: k19 sts, cast off 14 sts, k to end. Cont with this set of sts, leaving the others on a holder. P2 tog at neck edge on next row.
Row 2: k to last 9 sts, turn and p to end. Leave these sts on a holder and return to the others, joining yarn in at outer edge. K2 tog at neck edge on next row. Row 2: p to last 9 sts, turn work and k to end. Leave sts on a holder.

Right front
Using 5½mm needles and blue, cast on 28 sts. Row 1: k4, *p2, k2, rep from * to end. Row 2: *p2, k2, rep from * to last 4 sts, k4. Cont thus, in double rib, as for back, with a 4 st garter st border, ending with a WS row.
Change to 6½mm needles and cont in st st, inc 1 st at end of the first row and maintaining garter st border.
When work measures 14cm, ending on a WS row, **work pocket**: k8, slip the next 12 sts on to a holder and work the 12 pocket lining sts instead, k to end of row. Cont as before. When work measures 32cm, ending with a WS row, **work breast pocket**: as for first pocket. Cont as

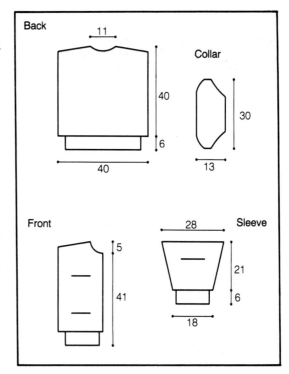

before until work measures 42cm, ending on a WS row.
Shape neck: cast off 6 sts, k to end. Now dec 1 st at neck edge on every row until 18 sts remain. Work straight until front measures 45cm, ending with a WS row. **Shape shoulder**: k to last 9 sts, turn and p to end. Leave sts on a holder.

Left front
As for right front, reversing out shapings and omitting the pockets.

Sleeves
Using 5½mm needles and blue, cast on 24 sts and work in double rib for 2 rows. Change to red and rib 2 rows. Change back to blue and rib until work measures 6cm.
Change to 6½mm needles and cont in st st, inc 1 st each end of next and every following 5th row until you have 36 sts. Next RS row **work pocket**: k11, slip the next 15 sts on to a holder and work the pocket lining sts instead, k to end. Cont shaping sleeve as before until you have 40 sts. Work straight until sleeve measures 27cm. Cast off loosely.

Materials
Melinda Coss chunky-weight wool – blue: 500gm; black: 50gm; red: 50gm; white: 50gm; gold and royal blue: less than 25gm of each.
One 42cm open-ended zip fastener.

Needles
One pair of 6½mm and one pair of 5½mm needles.

Tension
Using 6½mm needles and measured over st st: 14 sts and 19 rows = 10cm square.
N.B. Make every effort to keep your tension the same when working colour motif. Do not carry the base colour behind the mofit.

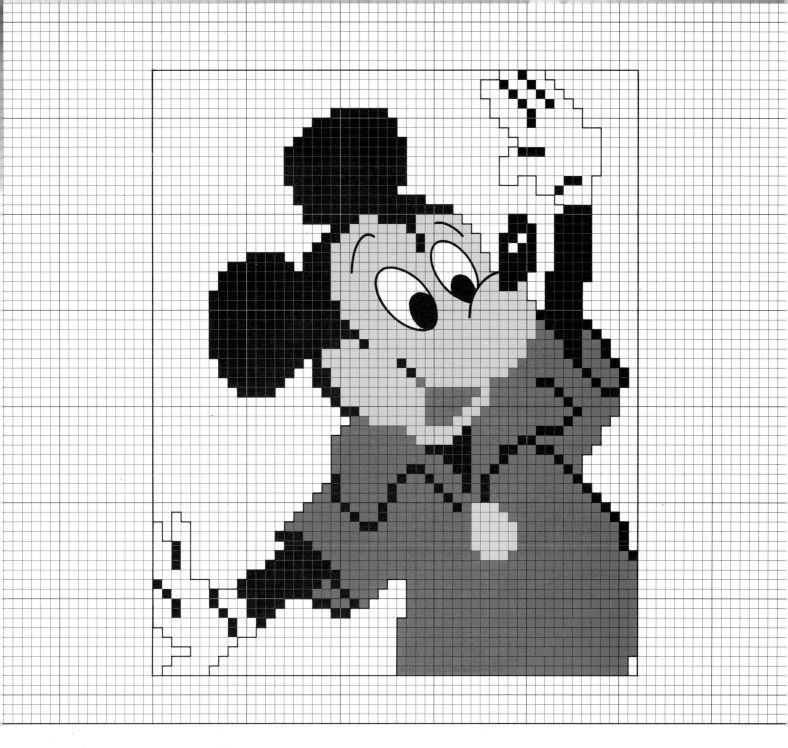

Collar

Using 5½mm needles and blue, cast on 4 sts.
Knit every row, inc 1 st each end of every alt
row, one st in from the edge, until you have 12
sts. Now work 1 edge straight while inc 1 st on
every row on the other edge until you have 18
sts. Work straight for 30 rows. Now shape the
other end to match, dec instead of inc until 4 sts
are left. Cast off.

Pocket borders

Using 5½mm needles and blue, work the held
sts above each pocket in k1, p1 rib, starting
with a RS row. Rib 1 row blue, one row red and
1 more row blue. Cast off knitwise, in blue,
taking care not to do so too tightly.

Making up

Knit both shoulder seams tog (*see* Techniques, pages 13-14). Slip stitch the side edges of the pocket borders to the main work, keeping them neat and straight.

Pin the zipper into position so that the front edges of the knitting barely touch one another. Using sewing thread, slip st the inner edges of the zipper to the inside of the knitting, taking care to work strong, firm sts that are not visible on the right side of the work.

Attach the collar with a flat seam, matching the cast off and cast on edges with the garter st front bands.

Open the work out and pin the sleeves to the body, taking care not to bunch or stretch them. Attach with a flat seam. Join the side and sleeve seams similarly.

Embroider the facial features as shown, using backstitch and satin stitch.

PLUTO MEN'S OR WOMEN'S SWEATER

A chunky-weight, roll-neck sweater for women or men. Pluto appears on the front, his bone on the back. The fit is very over-sized for women but a more standard fit for men (see diagrams for the actual measurements). The instructions are the same for women and men, except for the sleeves, which are quoted for women/men.

Back

Using 6½mm needles and base colour, cast on 88 sts.
Row 1: join in *natural k2, base colour p2, rep from * to end, loosely carrying the colour not in use at the back of the work. Row 2: *base colour k2, natural p2, rep from * to end, loosely carrying colour not in use at the front of the work. These 2 rows form the 2-tone double rib pattern. Work 6cm in rib, ending with a WS row.
Next row: using base colour only, k1, inc 1, k to last 3 sts, inc 1, k to end. Cont in st st, until work measures 26cm, ending with a WS row. Next row: k18, k first row of bone graph, k to end. Cont working the graph in this position until it is complete. Cont in base colour until work measures 80cm. Leave sts on a spare needle.

Front

As for back until you have worked the first 2 rows in st st.

Materials
Melinda Coss chunky-wool – blue: 1400/1500gm; natural: 150gm; beige: 200gm; contrasts: 50gm of each of the four colours, matched exactly to the graphs.

Needles
One pair of 6½mm needles and a set of double-pointed 6½mm needles.

Tension
Using 6½mm needles and measured over st st: 14 sts and 19 rows = 10cm square.
N.B. Make every effort to keep your tension the same when working the colour motifs. Do not carry the base colour behind the motif.

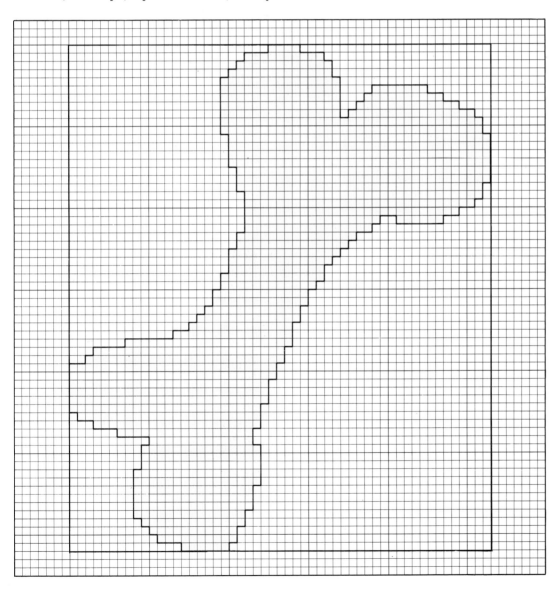

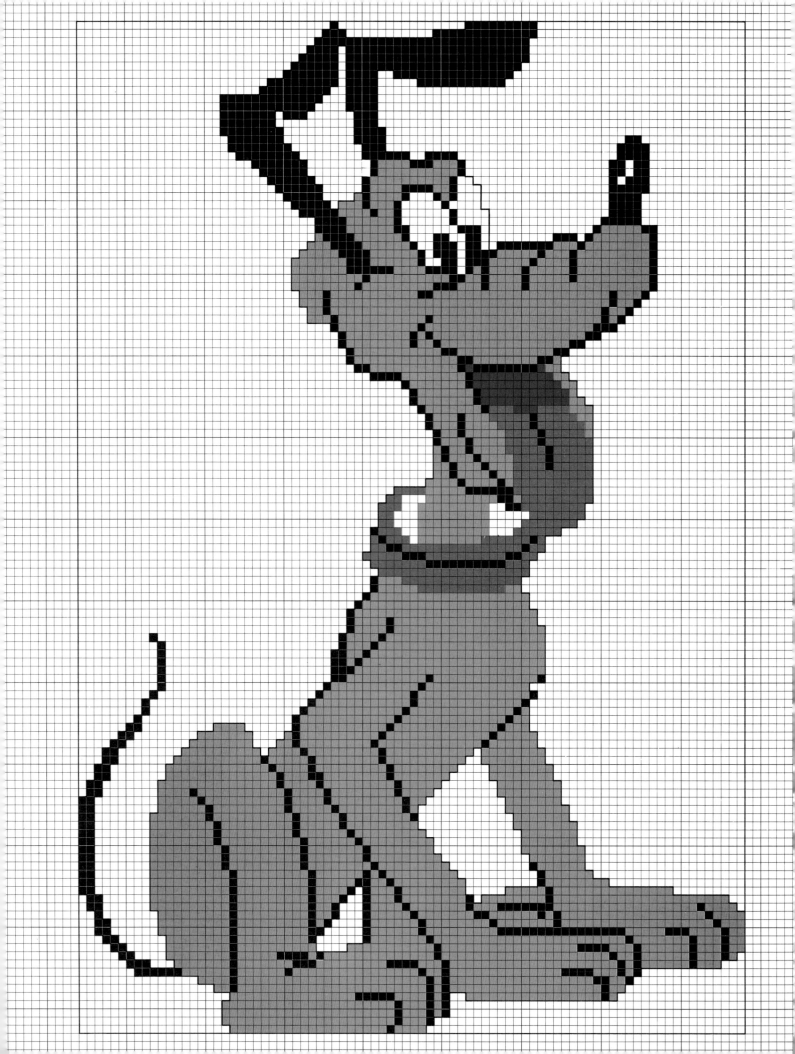

73

Next row: k3, k from first row of Pluto graph, k to end. Cont working the graph in this position until it is complete. Work 2 rows in base colour and then **shape neck**: work 40 sts, cast off 10 sts, work to end. Cont with this set of sts, leaving the others on a holder. Dec 1 st at neck edge on every row until 31 sts remain. Work straight until this side is as long as the back. Leave sts on a holder. Return to the other side of the neck and shape to match. Leave sts on a holder.

Sleeves

Using 6½mm needles, cast on 28/32 sts and work in 2-tone double rib for 5cm, ending with a WS row. Next row: knit in base colour, inc 4 sts evenly along the row from sts worked in base colour on the previous row (32/36 sts). Cont in base colour and st st, inc 1 st each end of next and every following 4th/5th row until you have 70 sts. Work straight until sleeve measures 41/49cm from beg. Cast off loosely.

Roll neck

Knit one shoulder seam tog, loosely cast off the 28 back neck sts, knit 2nd shoulder seam tog (*see* Techniques, pages 13-14). Using double-pointed 6½mm needles, base colour and with RS facing, knit up 11 sts down the left side of the neck, 10 sts across the front, 11 sts up the other side and 28 sts across the back (60 sts). Work in rounds of double rib for 12cm. Join in natural and purl the next row. Now rib 1 row and change back to base colour. Purl 1 row and then cont in rib for 2 more rows. Cast off in rib.

Making up

Join all seams with a very neat flat seam.

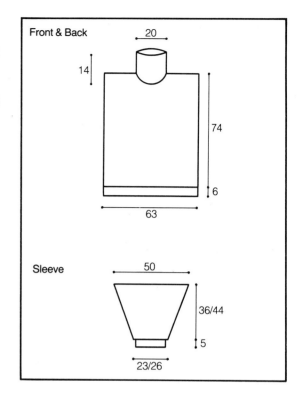

SNOW WHITE WOMEN'S SLIPOVER

A round-necked, sleeveless sweater worked in 4-ply wool, which may be worn as a twin set with the Seven Dwarfs Cardigan. The instructions are given for two sizes throughout, petite/small-medium (see diagram for actual measurements).

Back

Using 2¾mm needles and base colour, cast on 112/120 sts.
Row 1: *k1, p1, rep from * to end. Keep rep this row to form single rib until work measures 7.5cm. Next WS row, purl, inc into every 11th/12th st (122/130 sts).
Change to 3¼mm needles and knit the next row. Row 3: p21/25. MB (see Techniques, page 11), p79, MB, p to end. Work 3 rows in st st. Keep rep these 4 rows, keeping the bobbles in two straight lines for the entire length of the garment.
When 5/7 bobble rows have been completed, work 3 more rows in st st then work a horizontal band of bobbles thus: p5, *MB, p3, rep from * to last st, p1. Work another 55 rows (cont to work vertical bobble lines throughout), and then repeat the horizontal bobble band row. When work measures 35/37.5cm, **shape armholes**: cast off 5 sts at beg of next 2 rows and then dec 1 st each end of every row until 102/110 sts remain. Now work straight to 55 rows from the previous bobble band. Next row: p3, *MB, p3, rep from * to last 3 sts, MB, p2. Cont to work straight until work measures 52.5/55cm. Stop working the bobbles, cont in st st and **shape shoulders** (see Techniques, page 8).
Rows 1 and 2: work to last 10/12 sts, turn. Rows 3 and 4: work to last 19/22 sts, turn. Rows 5 and 6: work to last 28/32 sts, turn. Leave all sts on a spare needle.

Front

Work as for back until 8 rows have been worked after the first horizontal band of bobbles. Next row: k34/38, knit the first row from the graph, k to end. Cont working graph in this position until it is complete, meanwhile working the bobble grid around it – i.e., the grid forms a frame, the second horizontal band of bobbles stopping short of the first vertical line and starting up again the other side of the second vertical line so that it does not interfere with the motif.

Shape armholes: as for back and then work straight until the work measures 47/49cm, ending on a WS row.
Shape neck: k 41/45 sts, cast off 20 sts, work to end. Cont with this last set of sts, leaving the others on a holder. Dec 1 st at neck edge on every row until 34/38 sts remain. Now dec 1 st at this edge on every alt row until 28/32 sts remain. Work straight until work measures 52.5/55cm, ending with a WS row. Stop working bobbles and cont in st st. Next row **shape shoulder**: work to last 10/12 sts, turn and work to end. Row 3: work to last 19/22 sts, turn and work to end. Leave sts on a holder. Return to the other side of the neck and work to match, reversing out the shapings.

Neckband

Knit the left shoulder seam tog (see Techniques, pages 13-14). Using 2¾mm needles, slip the 46 sts at the back of the neck on to a needle and then, with RS of work facing, knit up 20/22 sts down the side of the neck, 20 across the front and 20/22 back up the other side (106/110 sts). Purl the first row, then work in single rib for 3cm. Cast off loosely in rib.

Armbands

Knit together the right shoulder and open out the front and back. Using 2¾mm needles and with RS facing, knit up 104/112 sts evenly along the left armhole from front to back. Purl the first row and then work in single rib for 3cm. Cast off loosely in rib. Work the right armband the same, knitting up the sts from the back to the front.

Materials

Melinda Coss 4-ply wool – green: 200/250gm; contrasts: less than 25gm of each of the 10 colours, matched exactly to the graph.

Needles

One pair of 3¼mm and one pair of 2¾mm needles.

Tension

Using 3¼mm needles and measured over stocking st: 28 sts and 36 rows = 10cm square.
N.B. Make every effort to keep your tension the same when working the colour motif. Do not carry the base colour behind the motif.

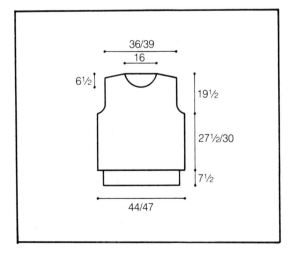

Making up
Use a flat seam for all ribbed parts, a narrow
backstitch elsewhere. Embroider Snow
White's facial features as shown.

SEVEN DWARFS WOMEN'S CARDIGAN

Materials

Melinda Coss 4-ply wool –
green: 400/450gm;
contrasts: less than 25gm of
each of the 15 colours,
matched exactly to the
graphs.
8 buttons.

Needles

One pair of 3¼mm and one
pair of 2¾mm needles.

Tension

Using 3¼mm needles and
measured over st st: 28 sts
and 36 rows = 10cm
square.
N.B. Make every effort to
keep your tension the same
when working the colour
motifs. Do not carry the
base colour behind the
motifs.

A round-necked, set-sleeved 1940s-style
cardigan, featuring the Seven Dwarfs set in a
grid of bobbles. Six dwarfs are worked on the
front, with Bashful hiding on the back. The
cardigan, which is knitted in 4-ply wool, is given
in two sizes, petite/small-medium.

Back

Using 2¾mm needles and base colour, cast on
118/126 sts.
Row 1: *k1, p1, rep from * to end. Keep
repeating this row to form single rib until work
measures 10cm. Next RS row: knit, inc into
every 10th/11th st (129/137 sts). Change to
3¼mm needles and cont in st st, working the
grid of bobbles from the graph but omitting the
dwarfs except for Bashful, who should be
worked in the same position as Grumpy is on
the front.
After working the 3rd horizontal band of
bobbles, work 4 more rows and then **shape
armholes**: cast off 5 sts at beg of next two rows.
Dec 1 st at each end of every row, 5 times
(109/117 sts). Cont to work straight until the 4th
horizontal row of bobbles has been completed.
Work 12/18 more rows. Leave sts on a spare
needle.

Right front

Using 2¾mm needles and base colour, cast on
57/61 sts and work in single rib for 10cm.
Next RS row: knit, inc into every 10th/11th st
(62/66 sts). Change to 3¼mm needles and work
from graph. After the 3rd horizontal row of
bobbles, work 3 more rows and then **shape
armhole**: cast off 5 sts at beg of next row and
then dec 1 st at this edge on every row for 5
rows (52/56 sts). Work straight to the point
where the neck shaping is indicated on the
graph. Next RS row **shape neck**: cast off 5 sts,
work to end. Now dec 1 st at neck edge on
every row until 32/36 sts remain. Work straight
until the front matches the back. Leave sts on a
spare needle.

Left front

As for right front, reversing out the shapings.

Sleeves

Using 2¾mm needles and base colour, cast on
57 sts and work in single rib for 7cm. Next RS
row: knit, inc into every 5th st (66 sts). Change
to 3¼mm needles and work a bobble grid as
for the back, positioning thus: row 1: p17, MB,
p31, MB, p17.
Keep working the grid, as set, working a
horizontal row as for the body but on the 9th
and every following 48th row. Meanwhile inc 1
st each end of every 25th/15th row, keeping all
new sts in the pattern as you go, but omitting
any bobbles that fall right at the edge of the
work. When there are 77/85 sts the sleeve
should measure 43/46cm. If short, work a few
rows straight to achieve the correct length.
Shape sleeve head: cast off 5 sts at beg of next
2 rows. Now dec 1 st each end of every row
until 61/63 sts remain. Dec 1 st each end of
every alt row until 31 sts remain. Cast off 4 sts at
beg of next 4 rows. Cast off remaining sts.

Front bands

Using 2¾mm needles and base colour, cast on
10 sts and work in single rib until the band is
long enough to fit from the bottom of the welt to
the front edge of the neck when very slightly
stretched. Leave the sts on a pin. Place a pin to
mark the first button position, 5 rows from the
cast-on edge. Divide the band equally and
mark 6 more button positions, making
allowance for the 8th being worked on the

The symbol "X" on the
graphs on pages 80 and 81
indicates that bobbles
should be worked at those
points; *see* Making a
bobble, page 11. The inner
line on the graphs is for the
petite size, the outer line for
the small-medium size.

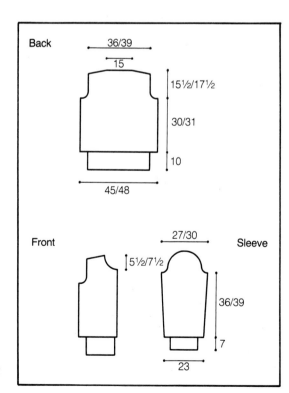

Back
36/39
15
15½/17½
30/31
10
45/48

Front
27/30   Sleeve
5½/7½
36/39
7
23

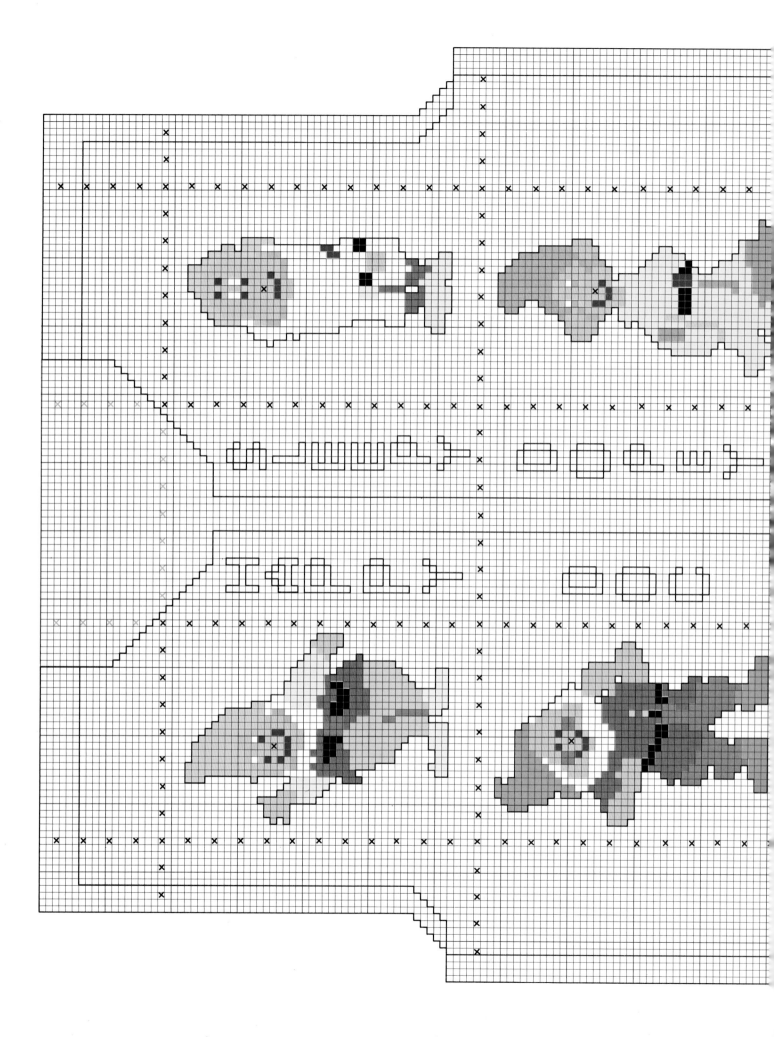

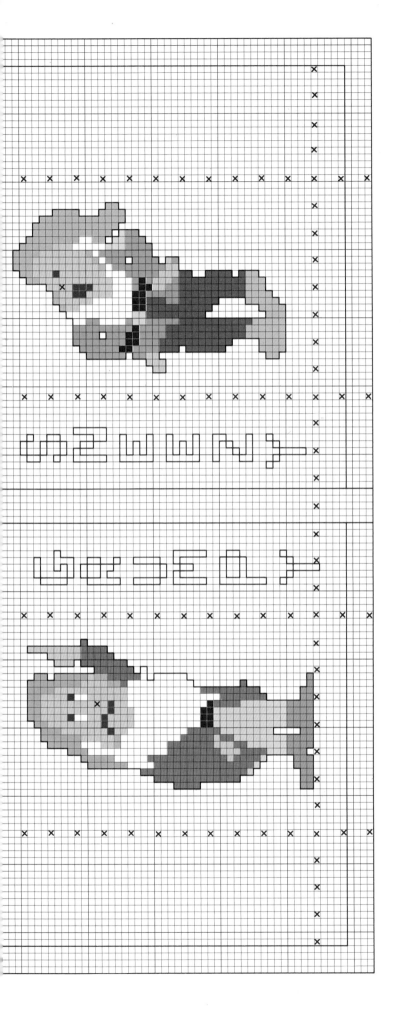
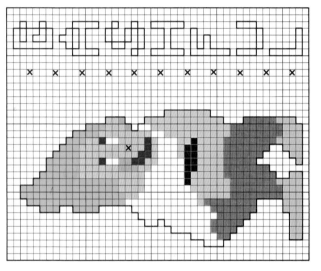

neckband. Now work the buttonhole band to match, working buttonhole rows to correspond to marker pins thus: rib 4, cast off 2, rib 4. On the next row cast on 2 sts above those that were cast off, and then cont normally to next buttonhole row. When this matches the first band, leave sts on a pin.

Neckband
Knit both shoulder seams tog (*see* Techniques, pages 13-14), and leave the central 45 back neck sts on a spare needle.

Using 2¾mm needles and base colour, rib the right-hand band sts on to the needle and with the RS of work facing, knit up 20/26 sts along right side of neck, knit the back neck sts on to the same needle and then knit up 20/26 sts down the left side of the neck, finishing by ribbing the right band sts (105/117 sts). Work in single rib for 3 rows. Work a buttonhole to correspond with the others. Rib 2 more rows and cast off in rib.

Shoulder pads
Using 3¼mm needles and 2 strands of base colour yarn, cast on 2 sts. Cont in garter st (knit every row), inc 1 st each end of every row until you have 26 sts. Now work straight for 4cm. Cast off. Work 2 the same.

Making up
Carefully pin the bands to the fronts, making sure that they are even. Attach with a flat seam. Join the side and sleeve seams with a flat seam over the ribs and a narrow backstitch over the pattern. Set the sleeves in last, distributing the sleeve head evenly around the armhole. Pin and backstitch.

Attach the buttons where the marker pins indicate and stitch the shoulder pads inside the cardigan as described on pages 15-16.

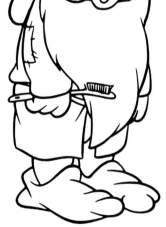

TWEEDLEDUM AND TWEEDLEDEE CARDIGAN

A V-neck "boxing" cardigan for men and women – the terrible twins battling it out on the front while the back is emblazoned with their names, in the prize-fighting tradition. Worked in double knitting wool, instructions are one-size women's/one-size men's, the raglan sleeves making it an easy-to-wear shape for anyone.

Back

Using 3¼mm needles and base colour, cast on 128/140 sts.
Row 1: *k1, p1, rep from * to end. This row forms single rib; work in exactly the same way wherever rib is required within the instructions.
Rib for 2cm, change to red and rib 2cm, return to base colour and rib 2cm. Change to 4mm needles and cont in st st until the work measures 29/31cm, ending with a WS row.
Next row: k24/30, k the first row from the lettering graph, k to end. Cont working graph as set until work measures 36/38cm, ending with a WS row.
Shape raglan (cont to work graph throughout): cast off 2 sts at beg of next 2 rows. Next row: k2, sl 1, k1, psso, k to last 4 sts, k2 tog, k2. Row 2: purl. Keep rep these two rows until the graph is complete. Now cont in base colour, shaping raglan as before until 36/42 sts remain. Work 3/4 rows straight. Cast off.

Right front

Using 3¼mm needles and base colour, cast on 62/68 sts and work in striped single rib, as for back, until work measures 6cm, ending with a WS row. Change to 4mm needles and work in st st for 4 rows.
Next row: k3/6, k the first row of the Tweedledum graph, k to end. Work graph in this position until it is complete. Meanwhile, when work measures 36/38cm, **shape raglan**: next WS row cast off 2 sts, work to end. Row 2: k to last 4 sts, k2 tog, k2. Row 3: purl. Keep rep these 2 rows until 52/58 sts remain.
Shape neck: dec 1 st at neck edge on next and every following 4th row, meanwhile cont to shape raglan as before. When 12/9 sts remain work the neck edge straight and cont to shape raglan until 4 sts remain.
Next row: purl. Row 2: k2, k2 tog. Row 3: purl. Row 4: k1, k2 tog. Work 2 rows straight. Cast off.

Left front

As for right front until the graph and then: k5/8, k first row of the Tweedledee graph, k to end. Now cont as for right front, reversing out the shapings and working the raglan decs as sl 1, k1, psso.

Sleeves

Using 3¼mm needles, cast on 52/58 sts and work in striped single rib, as for back, for 6cm. Change to 4mm needles and cont in st st, inc 1 st each end of next and every following 5th row, until there are 100/110 sts. Now work straight until the sleeve measures 43/50cm from the beg, ending with a WS row. **Shape raglan**: cast off 2 sts at beg of next 2 rows. Now dec 1 st each end of next and every following knit row, as on the back, until there are 12 sts left. Cast off.

Buttonband

Using 3¼mm needles and base colour, cast on 8 sts and work in single rib until the band is long enough to reach to the centre of the back neck when very slightly stretched. Leave on a pin. Divide the band into 4 sections from the very bottom to the point where the front neck shaping starts. Using safety pins, mark the

Materials

Melinda Coss DK wool – black: 550/600gm; red: 100gm; contrasts: less than 25gm of each of the 9 colours, matched exactly to the graphs.
Both sizes require 5 buttons.

Needles

One pair of 3¼mm and one pair of 4mm needles.

Tension

Using 4mm needles and measured over st st: 24 sts and 32 rows = 10cm square.
N.B. Make every effort to keep your tension the same when working the colour motifs.

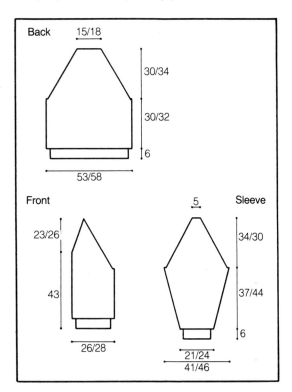

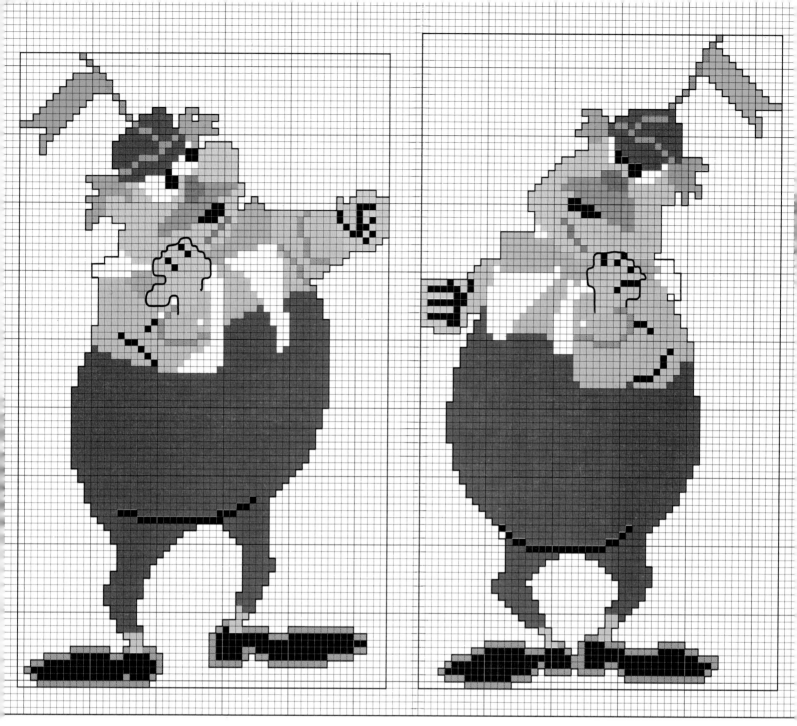

Tweedledum

Tweedledee

button positions, spacing them equally between the top and bottom positions.

Buttonhole band
Work as for the buttonband but working buttonhole rows where the marker pins indicate, thus: buttonhole row: rib 3, cast off 2, rib 3. Next row: rib, casting on 2 sts immediately above those cast off on the previous row.
Work the band until it is the same length as the other. Leave sts on a pin.

Making up
Throughout the seams are flat. Join the raglans first, followed by the sleeve and side seams. Now knit the two ends of the front bands tog, place this seam at the centre back neck of the cardigan and pin the bands to the fronts, taking care to distribute them evenly. Join with a very careful flat seam. Attach buttons where marker pins indicate.
Using backstitch, embroider the outline of the twin's fists in black yarn.

WINNIE THE POOH LAYETTE

An Eeyore dress, a Piglet cardigan and shorts outfit and a Pooh romper suit – all quoted in sizes for 6/9/12/18 month-old babies (see diagrams for sizing). All garments are worked in royal blue 4-ply wool, with contrast colours matched exactly to the graphs.

Materials

Melinda Coss 4-ply wool–
dress: 150/150/200/200gm;
cardigan: 150/150/150/150gm; **shorts:** 100/100/100/100gm; **romper suit:** 200/200/200/250gm; contrasts: less than 25gm of all contrast colours, matched exactly to the graphs.
The dress requires a few cm of thin pink ribbon and 30cm of black yarn for Eeyore's tail and bow; 2 snap fasteners and small metal buttons to stitch over them.
The shorts require ribbon elastic, 2cm wide, length to suit.
The cardigan requires 4 snap fasteners and small metal buttons to be stitched over them.
The romper suit requires 5 snap fasteners and small metal buttons to stitch over them.

Needles

One pair of 2¾mm, one pair of 3mm and one pair of 3¼mm needles.

Tension

Using 3¼mm needles and measured over st st: 28 sts and 36 rows = 10cm square.
N.B. Make every effort to keep your tension the same when working the colour motifs. Do not carry the base colour behind the motifs.

EEYORE DRESS

Back

Using 3mm needles and the base colour, cast on 124/132/140/148 sts.
Row 1: *k1, p1, rep from * to end. Keep rep this row to form single rib. Rib for 6 rows and then change to 3¼mm needles and cont in st st until work measures 25/27/29/31cm.
Next RS row: knit, working a dec every 3rd st (83/88/94/99 sts). Change to 3mm needles and work in k1, p1 rib for 5/6/7/8cm. **Shape armholes**: cast off 6/6/7/7 sts at beg of next 2

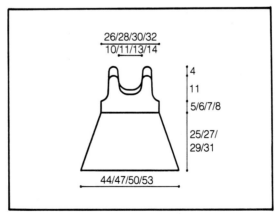

26/28/30/32
10/11/13/14

4
11
5/6/7/8
25/27/29/31

44/47/50/53

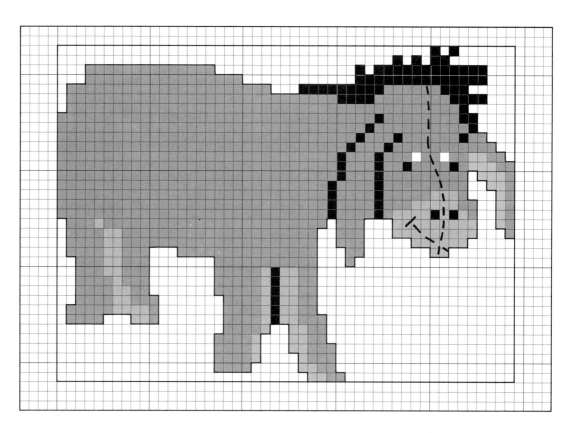

rows. Now dec 1 st each end of every row, 2 sts in from the edge and keeping in rib throughout until 63/68/72/77 sts remain. Work straight until work measures 12cm from beg of bodice rib. **Shape neck**: rib 23/24/25/26 sts, cast off 17/20/22/25 sts, rib to end. Cont with this set of sts, leaving others on a holder. Dec 1 st at neck edge, 2 sts in from edge, on every row until 18 sts remain. Cont straight, in rib, until the work measures 18/19/20/21cm from beg of bodice rib. Now dec 1 st each end of every row, 1 st in from edge, until 4 sts remain. Cast off normally (i.e., not in rib). Return to other side of neck and work to match the first side.

Front

As for back until work measures 6cm, ending with a WS row.
Next row: k66/72/78/84, knit from Eeyore graph, joining in colours as required. Knit to end. Cont to work graph in this position until it is complete. Now work as for back until the ribbed bodice measures 9/9/11/11cm. **Shape neck**: as for back but working each strap to a length of 14/15/16/17cm from beg of bodice ribbing before shaping the end.

Making up

Join sides with a flat seam. Attach snap fasteners to straps according to size, and stitch one button on top of each fastener. Cut three

10cm lengths of black yarn and knot them together at one end, plaiting the strands to form Eeyore's tail. Secure the end by tying a small length of pink ribbon into a bow and stitch through this bow with matching thread to prevent it from coming undone. Attach the tail to Eeyore's rear. Embroider the facial features, as illustrated, using backstitch.

PIGLET CARDIGAN
Back

Using 3mm needles and base colour, cast on 76/80/84/88 sts.
Row 1: *k2, p2, rep from * to end. Keep rep this row to form double rib for 2.5cm. Change to 3¼mm needles and cont in st st until work measures 27/28/29/30cm. Leave sts on a spare needle.

Left front

Using 3mm needles and base colour, cast on 36/40/40/44 sts and work in double rib for 2.5cm. Change to 3¼mm needles and cont in st st until the work measures 22/23/24/25cm, ending with a RS row. **Shape neck**: cast off 4 sts at the beg of the next row. Now dec 1 st at neck edge on every row until 21/23/24/26 sts remain. Leave sts on a spare needle.

Right front

As for left front until work measures 8cm, ending with a WS row. Next row: k5/7/7/9 sts, k the first row from the Piglet graph, k to end. Cont working the graph in this position until it is completed. Now cont in base colour st st until work measures 22/23/24/25cm, ending with a WS row. **Shape neck**: as for the left front. Leave sts on a spare needle.

Sleeves

Using 2¾mm needles and base colour, cast on 40/40/44/44 sts and work in double rib for 2 rows. **Change to fuchsia, knit 1 row, rib 1 row. Return to base colour, knit 1 row, rib 3 rows.** Rep from ** to **. Knit the next row, inc into every 5th/4th/5th/4th st (48/50/52/55 sts). Change to 3¼mm needles and cont in st st, inc 1 st each end of 3rd/6th/1st/3rd and every following 3rd/3rd/4th/4th row until you have 74/78/82/85 sts. Work straight until the sleeve measures 15/17/19/21cm. Cast off.

Neckband

Knit both shoulder seams tog (*see* Techniques pages 13-14), leaving the centre 34/34/36/36 back neck sts on a spare needle. Using a 2¾mm needle, base colour and with RS facing, knit up 18/18/21/21 sts around the right side of neck, knit the back neck sts on to the same needle and then knit up 18/18/21/21 sts down the right side of the neck. Work in double rib for 2.5cm. Cast off in rib.

Front bands

Using 2¾mm needles, base colour and with RS of the right front facing, knit up 74/78/82/86 sts evenly from the very bottom edge to the top edge of the neckband. Work in double rib for 2.5cm. Cast off in rib. Work the left front band to match.

Making up

Open out body and pin sleeves into position, taking care not to bunch them. Sew with backstitch. Join the sleeve and side seams with a flat seam over the ribs, backstitch over the st st. Attach the snap fasteners to the front bands and stitch a button on top of each. Embroider Piglet's facial features, as illustrated, using backstitch and satin stitch.

PIGLET SHORTS
Back

Start at the lower edge of the left leg. Using 3mm

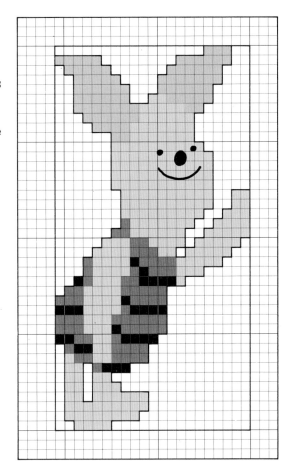

needles and base colour, cast on 32/36/36/40 sts. Work in double rib for 2 rows. Now work from ** to ** as for the cardigan sleeves twice. Rib 2 more rows. Knit the next row, inc into every 3rd/4th/4th/5th st (42/45/45/48 sts). Now change to 3¼mm needles and cont in st st, until work measures 10/11/12/13cm, ending with a WS row. **Shape crotch**: next row cast off 3 sts, work to

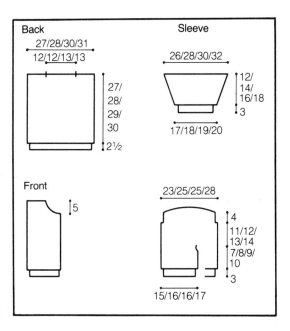

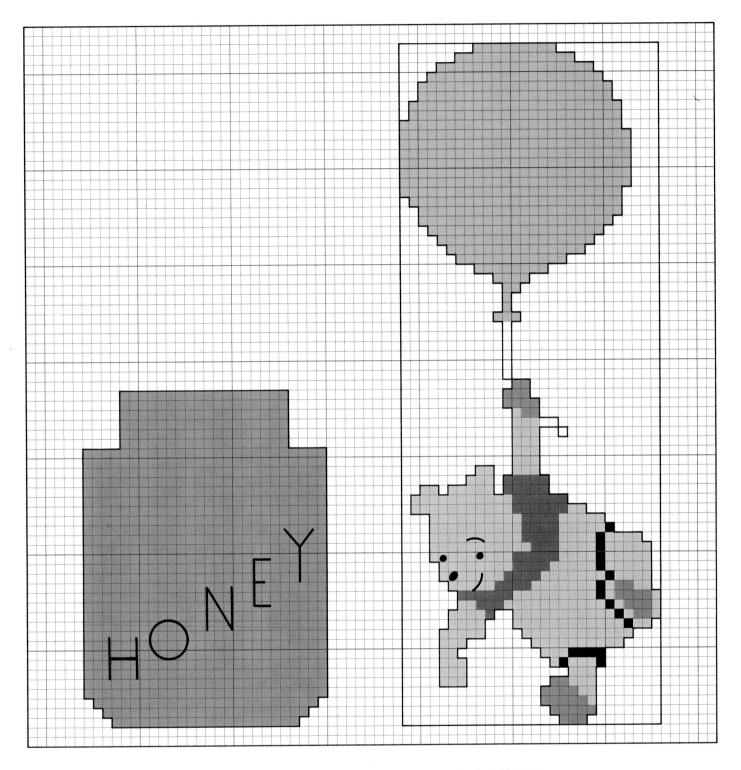

end. Dec 1 st at crotch edge on next 4 rows.
Leave these sts on a spare needle.
Work the right leg to match, reversing out the
shapings. Now slip the left leg sts on to the same
needle, crotch shapings to the centre of the row.
Next row (WS): purl. Row 2: k32/35/35/38, k2 tog
tbl, k2, k2 tog, k to end. Purl one row and then
knit the next row, dec 1 st either side of centre 2
sts as on row 2 (66/72/72/78 sts). Work straight
until work measures 21/23/25/27cm.

Shape waist: next row work to last 10 sts, turn
and repeat. 3rd row: work to last 20 sts, turn and
repeat. 5th row: work to last 30 sts, turn and
repeat. Break off yarn and slip all sts on to the
same needle. Now work across all sts, dec 1 st in
every 10 sts. Cont in st st for a further 16 rows.
Cast off.

Front
Work right leg as for back left leg until work

measures 10/11/12/13cm, ending with a RS row. **Shape crotch**: dec 1 st at crotch edge on next 4 rows. Leave these sts on a spare needle and work a left leg to match. Now work as for back, but dec 1 st each side of central 2 sts on 4 RS rows in all (64/70/70/76 sts). Cont as for back but omitting the turned rows.

Making up

Join seams with a flat seam, leaving the waist seam open for 2cm at the very top on one side. Turn in the cast off edge and slip st it down inside the waist to form a tube 2cm deep. Thread ribbon elastic through the opening that has been left and join the ends according to waist size.

POOH ROMPER SUIT

Back

Start at the lower edge of the left leg. Using 2¾mm needles and blue, cast on 32/33/35/36 sts and work in single rib for 5 rows. *Change to red and purl the next row. Work the following row in rib, as previously set. Change back to blue and purl the next row. Work 4 more rows in rib as previously set.* Rep from * to * once more. Work 5 more rows in rib and then change to st st, inc into every 3rd st (42/44/46/48 sts). Change to 3¼mm needles and cont in st st until work measures 17/18/19/20cm, ending with a WS row. **Shape crotch**: next row cast off 3 sts, work to end. Row 2: purl. Row 3: **k1, k2 tog, k to end.**

Rep last 2 rows (37/39/41/43 sts). Leave these sts on a spare needle.

Work the right leg to match, reversing out the shapings and dec by k2 tog through backs of loops (tbl). Now slip the left leg sts on to the same needle, crotch shapings to the centre of the row. Next row (WS): purl. Row 2: k34, k2 tog tbl, k2, k2 tog, k to end (72/76/80/84 sts). Work straight until work measures 32/34/36/38cm. Change to 2¾mm needles and cont in single rib for 3cm. Return to 3¼mm needles and cont in st st until work measures 38/40/42/44cm.

Form sleeves: cast on 33/36/39/42 sts at beg of next 2 rows. Now work straight until work measures 49/51/53/55cm. Next RS row **shape neck**: k54/58/62/66 sts, cast off 30/32/34/36 sts, k to end. Cont with this set of sts, leaving others on a holder. Dec 1 st at neck edge on next 2 rows. Work 2 rows straight. Leave sts on a holder. Return to the other side of neck and shape to match. Leave sts on a holder.

Left front

Work from bottom of left leg as for back of right leg until work measures 17/18/19/20cm ending with a RS row. Shape crotch: next row cast off 4 sts, work to end. Row 2: k to last 3 sts, k2 tog tbl, k1. Row 3: purl. Rep these last 2 rows another 2 times more (35/37/39/41 sts).

Cont as for back until work measures 38/40/42/44cm. **Form sleeve**: next RS row cast on 33/36/39/42 sts, work to end. Cont straight until work measures 44/46/48/50cm, ending with a RS

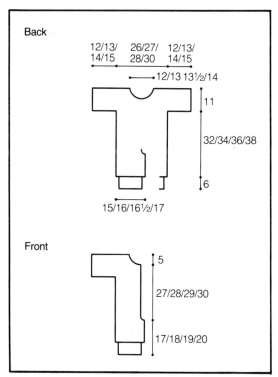

Back

12/13/14/15 26/27/28/30 12/13/14/15

12/13 13½/14

11

32/34/36/38

6

15/16/16½/17

Front

5

27/28/29/30

17/18/19/20

row. **Shape neck**: cast off 8 sts and work to end. Dec 1 st at neck edge on every row until 52/56/60/64 sts remain. Now work straight until the front matches the back. Leave sts on a holder.

Right front
This is worked as for left front, reversing out the shapings, but when work measures 9cm, ending with a WS row, incorporate the Winnie-the-Pooh graph. Next row: k8/9/10/11, work graph sts, joining in colours where necessary, k to end. Work graph in this position until it is complete and then cont as for left side.

Pocket
Using 3¼mm needles and tan yarn, cast on 20 sts. Work in st st, inc 1 st each end of every row for 3 rows. Now work straight until it measures 8cm. Next RS row: *k2 tog, k2, keep rep from * to end. Change to 2¾mm needles and work in single rib for 6 rows. Cast off normally (i.e., not in rib).

Front bands
Both knitted identically.
Using 2¾mm needles and base colour, with RS facing, knit up 82/86/90/94 sts along the straight edge of the front and work in single rib for 10 rows. Cast off normally (i.e., not in rib) but taking care to keep the tension correct so that this edge will not pull in.

Neckband
Knit one shoulder seam tog, cast off the 34/36/38/40 sts for the back neck and then knit the other shoulder seam tog (*see* Techniques, pages 13-14). Using 2¾mm needles and with RS of work facing, knit up 90/94/98/102 sts around the neckline from the outer edge of the right front band to the outer edge of the left front band. Purl the first row and then work 3 rows in single rib. Now work as for leg rib (page 90) from * to *. Cast off in rib.

Cuffs
Using 2¾mm needles, blue yarn and with RS facing, knit up 48/50/52/54 sts from back edge to front edge of cuff. Purl the first row and then work 3 rows in single rib. Now work as for leg rib (page 90) from * to * twice. Cast off in rib. Work left cuff the same, but knit up sts from front to back edge.

Making up
Join sleeve side and leg seams with a flat seam on ribs, a narrow backstitch over the st st. Overlap the base edges of the front bands and slipstitch these to the cast off edge at the crotch. Embroider the word "honey" on the pocket, as illustrated, using backstitch. Lightly press the pocket and then position on the breast, above the ribbing and carefully slipstitch around the edge.
Embroider Pooh's facial features, as illustrated, using backstitch and satin stitch.
Attach the snap fasteners, placing one at the neckband, one 5cm up from the base of the bands and spacing the others equally between. Stitch a button on top of each.

ABBREVIATIONS

alt	alternate(ly)
beg	begin(ning)
cm	centimetres(s)
cont	continue/continuing
dec	decrease/decreasing
inc	increase/increasing
k	knit
LH	left hand
MB	make bobble (*see* Techniques, page 11)
m1	make one – i.e., inc 1 st by working from the st below the next st to be worked
p	purl
psso	pass slipped stitch over
rep	repeat
rev st st	reverse st st
RH	right hand
RS	right side
sl	slip
st(s)	stitch(es)
st st	stocking stitch
tbl	through back of loop(s)
tog	together
WS	wrong side

YARN INFORMATION

All the sample garments illustrated in this book were knitted in Melinda Coss yarns. As many of the designs contain small quantities of several different colours, Melinda Coss offers individual kits containing only the quantities of yarn necessary to complete each garment. Each kit contains enough yarn to knit up to the largest size indicated on the pattern; in addition, zips, buttons, embroidery threads and trimmings are included where appropriate. Although authentic Disney approved colours must be used for the motifs, some designs may be knitted in a choice of background colours.

To order, simply contact Melinda Coss at No. 1 Copenhagen Street, London N1 0JB or telephone her on 01-833 3929.

For those who wish to substitute different yarns, weights are given throughout to the nearest 50g ball. To obtain the best results you must ensure that the tension recommended on your selected yarn *matches the tension* printed in our pattern. We cannot guarantee your results if this rule is not followed.